COLLINS GEM
CATS

COLLINS GEM
AST

P9-ANY-689

COLLINS GEM
HORSES
& PONIES

COLLINS GEM
INSECTS

COLLINS GEM
KINGS &
QUEENS

COLLINS GEM
MUSHROOMS
& TOADSTOOLS

a mine of information

COLLINS GEM
SNAKES

COLLINS GEM
SPIDERS

COLLINS GEM
STRESS
Survival Guide

COLLINS GEM
TAROT

a mine of information

COLLINS GEM
WINE
Guide

COLLINS GEM
WORLD
atlas

COLLINS GEM
YOGA

COLLINS GEM
ZODIAC
Types

a mine of information

COLLINS GEM

CRICKET

Jeff Fletcher

Authenticator: Ian Cole

HarperCollins*Publishers*

All photographs courtesy of Allsport except
for those on pages 99 and 145 courtesy of
Allsport/Hulton Getty Images; pages 15, 17,
24, 36, 100, 124, 125, 141 courtesy of Colorsport;
and page 62 courtesy of Ian Dobson Photography.
All illustrations courtesy of Foundry Arts.

All attempts have been made to contact the copyright
owners of material used in this book; in the event of
an oversight, the publishers will be glad to rectify any
omissions in future editions of this book

HarperCollins Publishers
PO Box, Glasgow G4 0NB

First published 1999

Reprint 10 9 8 7 6 5 4 3 2 1 0

© The Foundry Creative Media Co. Ltd 1999

ISBN 0 00 472340-6

Created and produced by Flame Tree Publishing, part of
The Foundry Creative Media Co. Ltd
Crabtree Hall, Crabtree Lane, London SW6 6TY

Special thanks to Mark Sandys and to Dave Jones.

Printed in Italy by Amadeus S.p.A.

 # Contents

Introduction

FIRST-CLASS CRICKET is likely to see a number of changes made to its structure and organisation over the next generation. There have already been moves to change the format of the County Championship, with Lord MacLaurin of Knebworth, Chairman of the England and Wales Cricket Board (ECB), seemingly determined to push through reforms that will hopefully bring commercial benefits to all levels of our national summer game.

In recent years we have witnessed players wearing coloured strips, playing under floodlights and ever-increasing sponsorship – to the extent that even the umpires' coats now carry a sponsor's logo.

The third umpire sits before a television monitor and officiates on certain close decisions and the one-day game continues to attract the paying customer, while the four-day Championship match is watched by just a handful of hardy enthusiasts.

The cricketing authorities are keen to encourage young people to take up the sport – and initiatives such as *Kwik Cricket* for boys and girls can only be beneficial to the sport.

The sporting landscape of the world is constantly shifting and cricket must evolve to keep up. Changes will come, but the essence of the game will not alter.

Cricket has a great tradition and that is one of its strongest assets. The game is still played by cricketers of all ages and abilities throughout the country and the legacy of the Hambledon club, W. G. Grace and other pioneers is safe.

How To Use This Book

THIS BOOK contains all the essential information that is needed to play, and understand, the game of Cricket. The origins of the game are explored, as is its current state. The most famous players, matches and incidents are recorded, and the backgrounds to the best-known competitions are looked at and the current statistics given. For those who would rather know how to play the game, and know what exactly the silly mid-off does and how to bowl like Shane Warne, there are two comprehensive instruction sections, detailing rules, techniques and tips for the would-be cricketer or those returning to the sport. A plan of the pitch showing the various positions is a vital tool to the further understanding of the game; this is given in the Laws of the Game section. To play cricket well requires some basic equipment with which to play – details of what exactly is needed are given.

Cricket is divided into nine sections, eight dealing with a different aspect of the game, with an extensive compendium section at the end. Each section is colour coded for easy reference. Part One deals with the History of the Game, looking back to its origins. Part Two looks at cricket in Britain: the competitions and winners. Parts Three, Four and Five look at the International game: both the nations that compete and at international competitions. Part Six details the best players both past and present and gives some current rankings. Part Seven is a guide to Playing the Game: where to play, tips on bowling, batting and fielding, and Part Eight takes a look at the Rules (simplified), how to score and the positions.

The Glossary is a useful summary of terms used in the book and the Useful Addresses section contains information on where to go for more information about all aspects of the game, such as the England & Wales Cricket Board. A comprehensive index will lead to you to the relevant information contained in the book.

A The page number appears in a colour-coded box indicating which part you are looking at.

B The aspect of the sport being dealt with is indicated at the head of the appropriate page.

C Instructive, interesting text gives all the essential information needed for the particular aspect of the sport.

D The topic covered on the page will be illustrated with clear photographs or diagrams, with identifying captions where appropriate.

HISTORY OF THE GAME
Early Cricket

Cricket has a long history and some forms of the game can be traced back hundreds of years. There is a record of King Edward I's household being involved in a game similar to cricket – with the Prince of Wales actively taking part.

SOME HISTORIANS HAVE even tried to find a line back to ancient civilisations such as the Egyptians. There will always be debate on the origins of cricket, but there does appear to be a consensus of opinion that suggests the game that

The Grace family in 1867.

HAMBLEDON, HANTS
THE CRADLE OF CRICKET.

A GRAND MATCH
WILL BE PLAYED ON
BROADHALFPENNY DOWN,
(the original Ground of the famous Hambledon Club of 1750).

On Sept. 10th, 11th, 12th.
HAMBLEDON
v.
ENGLAND

The following Members of the Hambledon Cricket Club have been selected to play against

MR. JESSOP'S ENGLAND ELEVEN:

E. Whalley-Tooker, Captain.   W. White.   W. Langridge.   Llewellin.
E. M. Sprott.   Captain E. G. Wynyard.   Mead.   Newman.
C. B. Fry.   A. J. Hill.   Stone.

On the first day of the Match, during Luncheon interval,

A ⋆ GRANITE ⋆ MEMORIAL
which has been erected to mark the site of the original Cricket Ground of the celebrated Club
of 150 years ago, will be unveiled by DR. W. G. GRACE.

Admission to the Ground will be Free, except to Horses, Vehicles and Cycles. Seating accommodation will be found up to an unlimited, but within a charge of 1/- will be made. Tickets can be obtained at either entrance or of Members of the Committee. Refreshments and Luncheons will be supplied on the Ground at a tariff appointed by the Committee.

Horses must be unharnessed at owner's risk, on that part of the Ground apportioned by the Committee, and with fodder supplied for that purpose.

THE BAND OF THE TRAINING SHIP "MERCURY" has been engaged to play on the Ground during the Match.

The London and South-Western Railway Company will issue Cheap Tickets from London and various stations to West Meon, Droxford, Farnham and Rowland's Castle, in connection with this Match. For particulars see Company's bills.

Any further particulars may be obtained from the Hon. Secretary, Mr. J. A. Barr, Hambledon.

P. O. BRIXEY, Printer, Hambledon.

Poster celebrating 150 years of cricket at Hambledon, 1908.

grew into the modern version of cricket originated in the sheep country of south-east England. A ball made of rag or wool would be bowled (or rolled) along the short, downland grass and the target would be the wicket-gate ('wicket') of the sheepfold. The 'batsman' would use his crook to hit the ball and that explains why early bats were long with a curved blade.

Hambledon is a name synonymous with the history of cricket. In the 1760s a club was formed in the Hampshire village bearing that name. It was run by wealthy patrons but its better cricketers were local craftsmen and farmers.

The game began to spread and towards the end of the eighteenth century cricket was being played regularly in the London area.

THE MCC IS ESTABLISHED

Another club vitally important to the story of cricket was formed in 1787 – the Marylebone Cricket Club (MCC). The club was set up after Thomas Lord had earlier established the first ground bearing his name at Dorset Square, London, in 1782.

THE MCC SOON BEGAN to revise the laws of cricket and became the sport's most important authority. Recent administrative changes have seen it lose some of its powers and the club embroiled in the vexed issue of female membership. On 28 September 1998, after a second ballot within eight months, 70 per cent of MCC members voted to allow women to become members – after 211 years of all-male membership. However, the club has probably been the single most important institution in the history of the game.

DEVELOPMENT OF THE GAME

AS THE GAME developed in the nineteenth century different bowling styles were tried. Originally, only underarm bowling was allowed until several bowlers began using the round-arm action, which was officially sanctioned in 1835. Bowlers then started to experiment with overarm actions and after some controversy this form of bowling was made legal on 10 June 1864. To many this date represents the start of cricket's modern era.

England v Australia, Lord's, 1930.

Pitches were better prepared towards the end of the century and batsmen began to build longer innings and the number of runs scored by each team increased.

The brilliant W. G. Grace, who made his first-class debut back in 1865, did not wait for improved playing conditions before he began transforming the art of batting. The 'Great

Doctor' completely dominated cricket during his playing career and remains the single most recognised figure in the game. It was his exploits that made cricket our summer sport and his larger than life personality that helped shape the game as we know it.

W. G. Grace.

Start of the County Championship in England and Wales

Matches played between county sides date back to the early eighteenth century. The earliest recorded match was between Kent and Surrey, played at Dartford in 1709.

THE FIRST COUNTY CHAMPIONSHIP MATCH

LOCAL BUSINESSMEN quickly saw the commercial potential of inter-county cricket matches in much the same light as prize-fighting and other crowd-pulling sporting events. The bigger the event, the bigger the purse and resultant public interest.

But as with the origins of the sport itself, cricket historians disagree on the actual date of the first County Championship. Details of results and Championship winners are sketchy and unreliable until 1890, when the Championship was formally constituted.

EARLY WINNERS

HITHERTO THERE WERE often differences of opinion between the contemporary cricket publications as to which county was entitled to be labelled 'champions'. There was a lack of formal rules to determine the title holders and the task of naming the county champions fell to cricket correspondents, who based their decision on the playing records of each team throughout the season. There was no official championship table, no organised fixture list and, as a consequence, much confusion. For example, some record

Surrey batsman, 1890s.

books show Derbyshire as winning the title in 1874 while others list Gloucestershire; in 1878 some records show the Championship as being 'undecided' while others name Middlesex as title winners.

Despite the ambiguity caused by a lack of formal County Championship rules and records for most of the nineteenth century, certain teams did emerge as the dominant sides of their era. For example, Kent were accepted as the leading county in the 1840s, followed in the next decade by Surrey. From the mid-1860s until the late 1880s Nottinghamshire reigned supreme, with only Gloucestershire offering much of a challenge.

THE CHAMPIONSHIP GAINS RULES

Rules governing playing qualifications were agreed in 1873 and some suggest County Championship winners should be recognised from that year. However, others argue that the most important development came as a result of a meeting of counties at Lord's in December 1889.

REPRESENTATIVES FROM Gloucestershire, Kent, Lancashire, Middlesex, Nottinghamshire, Surrey, Sussex and Yorkshire agreed on a method of deciding the Championship and only from 1890 could an official list of county champions commence.

After much meticulous research of the sporting press of the time, the late Rowland Bowen did have a list of 'acknowledged' county champions for the years 1864 to 1889 accepted by *Wisden Cricketers' Almanack*. Bowen named Surrey as the first county champions in 1864, but it must be emphasised the list has no official status. Surrey also beat the seven other founder members to win the first official County Championship in 1890.

A year later Somerset joined the Championship and in 1895, the inclusion of Derbyshire, Essex, Hampshire, Leicestershire and Warwickshire brought the number of competing counties up to 14. Worcestershire (1899), Northamptonshire (1905), Glamorgan (1921) and finally Durham (1992) have all been accepted into the Championship which now includes the 18 first-class counties of England and Wales.

J. T. Brown, Yorkshire cricketer, 1890s.

Start of Sunday League Cricket

The success of the Gillette Cup – the one innings, limited-overs competition introduced in 1963 – encouraged the authorities to look for another showpiece for the booming public interest in one-day cricket.

THE POPULARITY OF THE televised International Cavaliers XI matches was considered an addition to the more hard-nosed attitude required for success in local league cricket. The Cavaliers' matches were ideally packaged for television – each innings was expected to last two hours and the whole game from start to finish extended to just under four-and-a-half hours. The outcome of the deliberations saw the introduction in 1969 of a new Sunday League.

After detailed negotiations with the cricketing authorities, headed by S. C. Griffith, secretary of the newly-constituted Test and County Cricket Board (TCCB), Imperial Tobacco were awarded the contract to sponsor the new competition. It was to be called the John Player League and matches were to be shown live on BBC TV, who had won the broadcasting rights.

THE FIRST SUNDAY MATCHES

ALL 17 FIRST-CLASS COUNTIES at the time took part. Matches were played on

Sundays and started in the early afternoon to counter accusations that games commencing in the morning might discourage people from going to church. Each side bowled 40 overs and bowlers were restricted to a 15-yard run-up and allowed to bowl a maximum of eight overs. Four points were awarded for a win and two points for a tie. Two points were also awarded if rain or bad light prevented an outright result.

AXA Sunday League, 1996 (Yorkshire v Nottinghamshire).

HOW LONG SHOULD GAMES BE?

If bad weather did disrupt play, matches could be
rescheduled and staged over a minimum 10 overs.
Traditionalists were unhappy with this particular option,
which they saw as nothing more than a lottery – with
both sides expected to slog at almost every delivery.

IN 1993 MATCHES were extended to 50 overs per side, but
the experiment lasted for just one year and the following season
the 40 overs per side rule was reinstated.

CRICKET APPEARS ON TV

THE BBC TELEVISED AN entire live John Player League
match every Sunday from its inaugural season in 1969 until
1980. Coverage became more spasmodic after that but in
recent years a match was shown in full on a regular basis on
satellite television.

Refuge Assurance took over the sponsorship of the Sunday
League in 1987 and supported the competition for five
seasons. No commercial sponsor stepped forward for the 1992
season. AXA Equity & Law Insurance took over sponsorship in
1993 and continued to give its name to the League until 1998,
its final season.

Towards the end, the competition was known simply as
the AXA League because midweek matches were scheduled
and day/night games were also introduced. The bigger
counties experimented with the use of floodlights and the
response from the public was generally favourable.
Attendances at the day/night matches were encouraging, but
as with most aspects of cricket it all depended on good, dry
weather.

Warwickshire win the Sunday League, 1997.

Growth of
International Cricket

At the height of Britain's imperial powers in the
nineteenth century, the game of cricket was
introduced to the far-flung corners of the Empire,
mainly by the armed forces and sporting enthusiasts
from within the foreign civil service and expatriate
business communities.

A GOOD STANDARD OF cricket was played in Canada
and the USA towards the middle of the nineteenth
century. In fact, the first overseas tour by an English cricket
team was made to these two countries in 1859 under the
captaincy of Nottinghamshire's George Parr.

THE FIRST TOURS

WHEN REPORTS OF THE tour to North America reached
Australia, local businessmen quickly put their heads together
and arranged for a tour 'Down Under'. In 1861–62 an English
cricket tour party made the first of many subsequent tours to
Australia.

Within the next 30 years or so tour parties reached New
Zealand, South Africa and the West Indies. The first overseas
tour of England was made by a party of 13 Australian
Aborigines in 1868.

THE FIRST TEST MATCH

NINE YEARS LATER, the first-ever Test match was played
when England faced Australia at the Melbourne Cricket
Ground. Play started on 15 March 1877 and the first ball in

Test cricket was bowled by England's Alfred Shaw to Australian opening batsman Charles Bannerman the first run was scored by Bannerman off the second ball of the over. Yorkshire's Allen Hill took the first Test wicket when he bowled Nat Thomson, and Hill also held the first catch in Test cricket to send back number three batsman Horan.

West Indies v Australia, 1991.

AUSTRALIA WIN FIRST TEST

Bannerman retired hurt on 165, the first Test century and the only first-class hundred of his career. Australia went on to score 245 and secured a 49-run first-innings lead when they bowled out England for just 196.

ALTHOUGH ENGLAND bounced back and dismissed Australia for only 104 in their second innings, the home side won the inaugural Test match by 45 runs after the tourists could make just 108 all-out in the fourth innings.

At this moment international cricket was born with overseas tours and Test matches increasingly featured in the sporting calendar.

Warwickshire v Australia, 1899.

CRICKET IS REGULATED

THE BOARD OF CONTROL was established by the MCC in 1898 to oversee all aspects of Test cricket played in England. The Imperial Cricket Conference was set up in 1909 by founder members England, Australia and South Africa. The international body met regularly at Lord's to discuss all matters relating to the development of cricket and was administered by the MCC until 1993. The ICC kept its initials but was retitled the International Cricket Conference in June 1965, in July 1989 the organisation changed its name again to the International Cricket Council.

India, New Zealand and the West Indies were voted full members of the ICC in 1926 and became Test match-playing countries. In later years, Pakistan (1952), Sri Lanka (1981) and finally Zimbabwe (1992) joined the ICC to bring the number of countries currently playing Test cricket to nine.

England v India, third Test, 1996.

Women's Cricket

EARLY MATCHES

Women have been playing cricket since the middle of the eighteenth century. The earliest account of a match dates back to June 1745 when the Reading *Mercury* published a report on a game played between Bramley and Hambledon on Gosden Common, near Guildford, Surrey.

THE POPULARITY OF women's cricket spread through the south-east of England, especially in the counties of Surrey and Sussex. Women's country-house cricket flourished in late-Victorian and Edwardian times.

WCA IS ESTABLISHED

AFTER THE FIRST WORLD WAR, many of the larger public schools for girls started to play cricket. The need for a national administrative body became apparent and the Women's Cricket Association (WCA) was formed in October 1926. It accepted the MCC's Laws of Cricket with one exception – the ball to be used was smaller than in men's cricket.

A stalwart of the WCA was Netta Rheinberg, who was its long-serving secretary. She was also a noted writer and became the first broadcaster and commentator on women's cricket.

Australia (1931) was the first of many other countries to form their own authorities as organised women's cricket developed throughout the world.

The International Women's Cricket Council (IWCC) was formed in 1958 to administer tours between member countries and form a single mouthpiece for the sport worldwide.

CRICKET GOES ON TOUR

THE FIRST OVERSEAS tour by a women's cricket team saw England travel to Australia and New Zealand in 1934–35. That tour included the first women's Test match played at Brisbane in December, in which England beat Australia by nine wickets.

In the same series, England's Myrtle Maclagan scored the first century in women's Tests, when she hit 119 in the second Test at Sydney on 7 January 1935. Maclagan and Molly Hide, who captained England from 1937 to 1954, were the stars of the game.

Jan Brittin playing for England v Australia, 1998.

GREAT FEMALE PLAYERS

After the Second World War, England produced another outstanding player – Mary Duggan, a great batswoman and slow left-arm bowler.

OTHER COUNTRIES ALSO had their star players and Australia's Betty Wilson was held in such high esteem that in 1985 she became the first woman to be awarded a place in her country's 'Sports Hall of Fame'.

Rachel Heyhoe-Flint, who captained England between 1966 and 1977 without defeat, is probably the best-known figure in women's cricket. Since retiring from the game she has become a successful broadcaster, writer and public relations officer. She remains a great champion for the sport and in recent times has been a leading campaigner in women's successful attempt to become members of the MCC. She hit the first six in official women's Tests – against Australia at the Oval in 1963. Between 1960 and 1979, she played 22 Tests for England and scored 1,594 runs, with four centuries, at an average of 45.54.

England's Jan Brittin is another excellent batswoman of recent years and in 1998 became the highest runscorer in women's Tests when she took her total to 1,935 runs before announcing her retirement after 19 years as an England player.

England won the first Women's World Cup in 1973 and claimed the trophy again in 1993. Australia won the title in 1978, 1982, 1988 and 1997.

Rachel Heyhoe-Flint.

Sponsorship and Cricket Today

Sponsorship, as is the case in all professional sport nowadays, is a vital source of income for the cricketing authorities.

I N ENGLAND THE money received from the major sponsors of Tests, one day internationals and the domestic

Mike Atherton lifting the Texaco trophy for England, 1997.

competitions is managed by the England and Wales Cricket Board and shared out between the 18 counties.

This revenue is crucial for the survival of the counties as local sponsorship and other money earned, such as gate receipts, falls far short of the cost of running a first-class county club.

EARLY SPONSORSHIP

SPONSORSHIP IS NOT a new phenomenon. The first English touring party to Australia in 1861–62 received financial backing from a Melbourne firm of caterers, Spiers and Pond. Nobody in those far-off days could have anticipated the way sponsorship would develop.

Even before big companies began sponsoring the major trophies, individual deals were negotiated to take full advantage of a top cricketer's image. In the 1950s, the dashing Denis Compton was seen in advertisements for Brylcreem hair products.

THE GILLETTE CUP

THE GILLETTE CUP was the first high-profile sponsored tournament in England. The limited-overs competition was introduced in 1963 and proved a popular event for both paying customers and those watching on television – a target audience for the sponsors.

Gillette were pleased with the exposure their brand name received in the early days, but ended their sponsorship of the Cup in 1980 when they felt that in the public's mind the word 'Gillette' conjured up visions only of a limited-overs cricket match – and not a range of shaving equipment.

THE NATWEST TROPHY

The National Westminster Bank took over the sponsorship in 1981 and have supported the NatWest Trophy ever since.

Essex win the NatWest trophy, 1997.

THE CORNHILL INSURANCE Company have enjoyed a long and successful sponsorship of England's home Test matches, while Britannic Assurance have lent their name to the County Championship since 1984.

The new commercial reality of sponsorship has not always been embraced by some of the more traditional elements in cricket and the media. Wisden's review of the 1963 Gillette Cup did not mention the sponsor's name and referred to the competition as 'The Knock-Out Cup'. Even today, some newspapers are loath to print a sponsor's name.

SPONSORSHIP TODAY

THE SUCCESS OF The early sponsorship deals led to the marketing men looking for every possible outlet for branding. Nowadays, you can see a sponsor's name printed on the field of play behind the bowler's run-up – this is done to maximise exposure to the television audience. The stumps, playing kit, equipment and even the umpires' coats all carry logos from sponsoring organisations.

Sponsorship is not only vital at first-class level; many amateur leagues are grateful for the support of local businesses. A club may also appreciate the sponsorship of a small local firm, such as a garage.

Sponsorship – not always greeted with open arms by all those concerned with cricket – is here to stay and the only question is which other aspects of the game can be targeted by the marketing men?

The Texaco trophy, 1996: England v India.

DOMESTIC COMPETITIONS

Britannic Assurance Championship

The County Championship is by far the oldest domestic competition in English cricket and dates back to the middle of the nineteenth century, although most cricket historians argue that the competition officially started in 1890 when the rules and regulations were formally constituted.

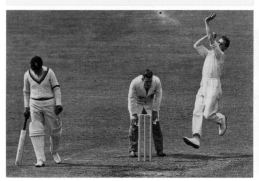

Surrey defeat Derby at the Oval, 1949.

T HE CHAMPIONSHIP is the most important title for a
county to win as many see the competition as the best
examination of a side's all-round strength. All 18 counties play
each other once a season over four days and both sides can bat
for a maximum of two innings.

Until 1998 the three other trophies contested by the first-
class counties – the NatWest Trophy, Benson and Hedges Cup
and the AXA Life League – were all competitions involving
one-day matches. The oldest of them – the NatWest Trophy,
formerly known as the Gillette Cup – dates back some 35 years,
a comparatively short time in the long history of cricket.

There is time to build an innings in county cricket and
many feel this form of the game gives a young player a better
grounding for Test match cricket than the limited-overs variety.

However, one of the problems for the counties is that
Championship matches attract few paying customers
through the turnstiles and there seems little interest by the

broadcasting
companies in the
four-day
competition.
One-day cricket
is easily packaged
for television,
whereas the
Championship is
seen by the
broadcasters as
the less attractive
version.

Nottinghamshire v Surrey, 1998.

The County Championship

There have been many attempts over the years to change the format of the County Championship. Matches were played over three days until recently when the authorities added another day in the hope of encouraging young batsmen and bowlers, especially spinners, to develop their skills.

T HE COVERING OF pitches from the elements is another bone of contention with many – certainly spin bowlers, whose effectiveness appears to have declined since the days of uncovered wickets.

The Championship has produced some wonderful cricket over the seasons with great county sides monopolising the title for lengthy periods, as Surrey did in the 1950s and Yorkshire in

Surrey County Cricket Club, 1959.

the 1960s. Strangely, it has been the less glamorous counties such as Leicestershire and Glamorgan who have won the Championship in recent years. Critics claim that these sides were least bothered by Test calls and make an argument for fewer Championship matches to be played so that clashes with Tests can be avoided.

There is much current debate about further and more fundamental reform of the County Championship. The ECB is anxious to introduce change for the good of the game, but many of the counties have resisted. Ideas such as splitting the Championship into two divisions or playing on a zonal basis have been suggested. Nobody is sure at the moment what the future holds. But one thing is certain – a successful longer version of the game is vital for the long-term health of cricket, and the England team.

Brian Lara (Warks) with his world record score of 501 not out v Durham, 1994.

Official Champions Since the Second World War

1946	Yorkshire
1947	Middlesex
1948	Glamorgan
1949	Middlesex/Yorkshire (joint winners)
1950	Lancashire/Surrey (joint winners)
1951	Warwickshire
1952	Surrey
1953	Surrey
1954	Surrey
1955	Surrey
1956	Surrey
1957	Surrey
1958	Surrey
1959	Yorkshire
1960	Yorkshire
1961	Hampshire
1962	Yorkshire
1963	Yorkshire
1964	Worcestershire
1965	Worcestershire
1966	Yorkshire
1967	Yorkshire
1968	Yorkshire
1969	Glamorgan
1970	Kent
1971	Surrey
1972	Warwickshire

Warwickshire celebrate their 1994 victory.

1973	Hampshire
1974	Worcestershire
1975	Leicestershire
1976	Middlesex
1977	Middlesex/Kent (joint winners)
1978	Kent
1979	Essex
1980	Middlesex
1981	Nottinghamshire
1982	Middlesex
1983	Essex
1984	Essex
1985	Middlesex
1986	Essex
1987	Nottinghamshire
1988	Worcestershire
1989	Worcestershire
1990	Middlesex
1991	Essex
1992	Essex
1993	Middlesex
1994	Warwickshire
1995	Warwickshire
1996	Leicestershire
1997	Glamorgan
1998	Leicestershire

Leicestershire take the 1998 championship.

Final 1998 Britannic Assurance Championship Table

	P	W	L	D	Batting	Bowling	Points
Leicestershire	17	11	0	6	47	51	292
Lancashire	17	11	1	5	30	56	277
Yorkshire	17	9	3	5	47	63	269
Gloucestershire	17	11	5	1	23	65	267
Surrey	17	10	5	2	38	57	261
Hampshire	17	6	5	6	27	61	202
Sussex	17	6	7	4	30	63	201
Warwickshire	17	6	8	3	35	60	200
Somerset	17	6	7	4	30	54	192
Derbyshire	17	6	7	4	28	55	191
Kent	17	5	5	7	18	59	178
Worcestershire	17	4	6	7	32	59	176
Glamorgan	17	4	6	7	36	55	176
Durham	17	3	9	5	30	65	158
Northamptonshire	17	4	5	8	31	52	146*
Nottinghamshire	17	3	10	4	20	60	140
Middlesex	17	2	9	6	28	52	130
Essex	17	2	11	4	16	58	118

* Northamptonshire deducted 25 points for preparing
  unfit wicket.

Top eight counties qualify for 1999 Super Cup competition.

Leicestershire win the County Championship trophy, 19

WOODEN SPOONS

MANY PEOPLE were shocked to see Middlesex and Essex finish at the foot of the 1998 table. Since 1895, when the Championship was expanded from nine to 14 teams, Essex had finished bottom of the Championship only once before, in 1950. Middlesex have never finished bottom, although they came perilously close in 1998. Lancashire and Surrey are the only other counties not to have finished in last position. Derbyshire, Northamptonshire and Somerset have all ended the season with the 'wooden spoon' on 11 occasions.

Sunday League Championship

Lancashire won the first John Player Sunday League in 1969 under their inspirational captain, Jackie Bond. The Red Rose county were a very successful one-day outfit between 1968 and 1972 and the epitome of the modern one-day side. They had a number of solid all-rounders and, crucially, athletic and enthusiastic fielders.

COMPREHENSIVE TELEVISION coverage on BBC2 gave the competition a great early boost and it soon became popular with the paying public. Whole families would attend these afternoon matches, their short duration allowing time for the morning's domestic chores and some relaxation in the evening. The successful counties in the League's early years, such as Lancashire and Kent attracted huge crowds to their home matches.

The matches, however, were not always popular with the players. Fast bowlers in particular felt at a disadvantage. Owing to pressure of time, their run-ups were restricted to 15 paces and during the run chase at the end of an innings a Test pace bowler, who would be straining for speed off his shortened run-up, could be bowling with no close fielders. The restrictions on the run-up were later removed, but that is the nature of the one-day game and it is what the public seems to desire. Over the seasons they have certainly seen some exciting cricket.

Yorkshire v Kent at Leeds, 1997 Sunday League.

SUNDAY LEAGUE PERFORMANCES

There have been 49 tied matches, with Worcestershire being involved in 11.

SURREY'S ALISTAIR BROWN hit the highest score in the League, making 203 against Hampshire at Guildford in 1997. Former Essex and England star Graham Gooch has been the most successful batsman in the competition, scoring 8,573 runs – with 12 centuries. In 1991 Worcestershire's Australian Test player Tom Moody hit the highest number of runs in a season – 917. Typically, Ian Botham left his mark on the competition by hitting 13 sixes in an innings for Somerset against Northamptonshire at Wellingborough School in 1986.

Former Essex and England left-arm pace bowler, John Lever, has taken the most wickets – 386. Another Essex player, Keith Boyce, claimed the best bowling figures of 8 for 26 against Lancashire at Old Trafford in 1971. The most economical bowling figures returned were by Somerset's Brian Langford. He completed his spell against Essex at Yeovil in 1969 with the incredible figures of 8-8-0-0. Not to have conceded a single run in eight overs during a one-day match was an astonishing performance.

Dominic Cork suffered a different fate when bowling for Derbyshire against Nottinghamshire at Trent Bridge in 1993. The England pace man finished with figures of 8-0-96-1 when he took his sweater from the umpire. In terms of games won, Kent have been the most successful team in the League, having claimed 264 victories in 487 matches played.

Warwickshire win v Gloucestershire at Edgbaston, 1997 Sunday League.

Sunday League
Championship Winners

John Player
County League

1969	Lancashire

John Player League

1970	Lancashire
1971	Worcestershire
1972	Kent
1973	Kent
1974	Leicestershire
1975	Hampshire
1976	Kent
1977	Leicestershire
1978	Hampshire
1979	Somerset
1980	Warwickshire
1981	Essex
1982	Sussex
1983	Yorkshire

John Player Special League

1984	Essex
1985	Essex
1986	Hampshire

Refuge Assurance League

1987	Worcestershire
1988	Worcestershire
1989	Lancashire
1990	Derbyshire
1991	Nottinghamshire

TCCB Sunday League

1992	Middlesex

AXA Equity
& Law League

1993	Glamorgan
1994	Warwickshire
1995	Kent
1996	Surrey

AXA Life League

1997	Warwickshire
1998	Lancashire

Final 1998 AXA Life League Table

	P	W	L	T	NR	Points	Run rate
Lancashire	17	12	2	0	3	54	12.18
Warwickshire	17	9	5	0	3	42	4.23
Essex	17	9	5	1	2	42	1.27
Leicestershire	17	9	6	0	2	40	15.13
Kent	17	8	6	0	3	38	1.19
Gloucestershire	17	7	6	0	4	36	−1.65
Worcestershire	17	7	6	1	3	36	−4.60
Hampshire	17	8	8	0	1	34	0.95
Yorkshire	17	8	8	0	1	34	−2.47
Glamorgan	17	7	8	0	2	32	−0.25
Nottinghamshire	17	7	8	1	1	32	−0.67
Middlesex	17	7	8	0	2	32	−4.90
Northamptonshire	17	6	7	1	3	32	2.80
Somerset	17	6	8	1	2	30	−0.10
Derbyshire	17	6	8	0	3	30	−5.10
Sussex	17	6	9	0	2	28	−1.84
Durham	17	4	9	1	3	24	−7.89
Surrey	17	3	12	0	2	16	−8.17

Lancashire win the AXA Sunday League, 1998.

NatWest Trophy

The NatWest Trophy began life as the Gillette Cup back in 1963 and is the oldest one-day competition in domestic cricket. In fact, the durable competition has seen off its younger rivals the AXA Life League (1969) and the Benson and Hedges Cup (1975). Both competitions were contested for the last time in 1998.

Waiting for play to begin is highly stressful for opening batsmen

THE FIRST-EVER Gillette Cup match took place between Lancashire and Leicestershire at Old Trafford on 1 May 1963 and was a preliminary tie to reduce the county teams involved to 16. Typically, rain intervened and the match went into a second day. For the record, Lancashire

(304-9) defeated Leicestershire (203) by 101 runs.

Sussex beat Worcestershire by 14 runs to win the first Gillette Cup Final in front of a packed house at Lord's on 7 September 1963. Interestingly, the most economical bowling figures came from the slow bowlers, Worcestershire's left-arm spinners Norman Gifford and Doug Slade and Sussex's off-spinner, Alan Oakman. Although on the losing side, Gifford went on to become the first Gillette Cup Final 'Man of the Match'.

Limited-overs cricket had certainly announced its arrival and within ten years the first one-day international, between England and Australia, was played. Cricket would never be the same again.

Gillette gave up their sponsorship in 1980 and the following year the competition became known as the NatWest Trophy.

The NatWest trophy final, 1998 (Lancashire v Derby).

NATWEST PERFORMANCES

There have been some heroic performances in the competition by both individuals and teams. Graham Gooch has dominated the NatWest Trophy, a feat he repeated in the other one-day competitions. The former Essex and England batsman hit 2,547 runs, scoring six centuries.

Alvin Kallicharan playing for Warwickshire.

ALVIN KALLICHARAN recorded the highest individual score – the former West Indies Test player struck 206 for Warwickshire against Oxfordshire at Edgbaston in 1984. Geoff Boycott holds the record for the highest individual score in the final. The former Yorkshire and England opener surprised onlookers with a scintillating 146 against a demoralised Surrey attack in the 1965 final and guided his side to victory by 175 runs.

Michael Holding (Derbyshire and West Indies) returned the best bowling figures – 8 for 21 off 10.1 overs against Sussex at Hove in 1988. Lancashire's former off-spinner Jack Simmons has the most economical figures. 'Flat Jack' finished with figures of 12-9-3-1 at the end of his spell against Suffolk

at Bury St Edmunds in 1985.

Somerset's Graham Rose hit the fastest century in the competition, reaching three figures off only 36 balls when playing against Devon at Torquay in 1990.

Wasim Akram lifts the NatWest trophy for Lancashire, 1998.

MINOR COUNTIES' PERFORMANCES

MINOR COUNTIES' TEAMS have been invited to take part in the competition since 1964 and there have been a number of giant-killing feats. Durham (twice), Hertfordshire (twice), Lincolnshire, Shropshire, Buckinghamshire and Cheshire have all beaten first-class opposition. Hertfordshire's second victory – against Derbyshire at Bishop's Stortford in 1991 in a bowling contest after the match was abandoned because of rain – was perhaps the strangest victory.

Gillette Cup Winners

(NatWest Trophy's former name)

1963	Sussex – beat Worcestershire by 14 runs
1964	Sussex – beat Warwickshire by eight wickets
1965	Yorkshire – beat Surrey by 175 runs
1966	Warwickshire – beat Worcestershire by five wickets
1967	Kent – beat Somerset by 32 runs
1968	Warwickshire – beat Sussex by four wickets
1969	Yorkshire – beat Derbyshire by 69 runs
1970	Lancashire – beat Sussex by six wickets
1971	Lancashire – beat Kent by 24 runs
1972	Lancashire – beat Warwickshire by four wickets
1973	Gloucestershire – beat Sussex by 40 runs
1974	Kent – beat Lancashire by four wickets
1975	Lancashire – beat Middlesex by seven wickets
1976	Northamptonshire – beat Lancashire by four wickets
1977	Middlesex – beat Glamorgan by five wickets
1978	Sussex – beat Somerset by five wickets
1979	Somerset – beat Northamptonshire by 45 runs
1980	Middlesex – beat Surrey by seven wickets

NatWest Trophy Winners

1981   Derbyshire – beat Northamptonshire by having taken more wickets after the scores finished level

1982   Surrey – beat Warwickshire by nine wickets

1983   Somerset – beat Kent by 24 runs

1984   Middlesex – beat Kent by four wickets

1985   Essex – beat Nottinghamshire by one run

1986   Sussex – beat Lancashire by seven wickets

1987   Nottinghamshire – beat Northamptonshire by three wickets

1988   Middlesex – beat Worcestershire by three wickets

1989   Warwickshire – beat Middlesex by four wickets

1990   Lancashire – beat Northamptonshire by seven wickets

1991   Hampshire – beat Surrey by four wickets

1992   Northamptonshire – beat Leicestershire by eight wickets

1993   Warwickshire – beat Sussex by five wickets

1994   Worcestershire – beat Warwickshire by eight wickets

1995   Warwickshire – beat Northamptonshire by four wickets

1996   Lancashire – beat Essex by 129 runs

1997   Essex – beat Warwickshire by nine wickets

1998   Lancashire – beat Derbyshire by nine wickets

1998 Final at Lord's; 5 and 6 September

Derbyshire 108 (36.4 overs. Martin 4 for 19). Lancashire 109-1 (30.2 overs). Lancashire won by nine wickets. Man of the Match: I. D. Austin.

Benson and Hedges Cup

Ray Illingworth was the first captain to raise aloft the Benson and Hedges Cup when his Leicestershire side beat his former county, Yorkshire, by five wickets in the inaugural final at Lord's in 1972.

TWENTY-SIX YEARS LATER, Paul Prichard was the last winning skipper to be presented with the trophy when Essex trounced Leicestershire by 192 runs in a final spoilt by rain and played over two days at Lord's on 11 and 12 June. Essex's name will be the last to be engraved on the trophy as 1998 saw the last Benson and Hedges Cup final.

The recently-retired Essex stalwart Graham Gooch did not play in the 1998 final, but over the years he has dominated the competition. He scored 5,176 runs in the Benson and Hedges Cup – over 2,000 more than any of his rivals. The former England captain has collected 22 Gold Awards over the years, but surprisingly has won only one winner's medal – in 1979, when he scored 120 out of his side's total of 290 for 6 against Surrey.

He also made the highest individual score in the competition – 198 not out against Sussex in 1982. Essex also hit the highest-ever total – 388 for 7 against Scotland at Chelmsford in 1992.

Only two other players have made centuries in Benson and Hedges Cup finals. They are Somerset's Viv Richards, who made 132 against Surrey in 1981, and Kent's Aravinda de Silva, who made 112 from 95 balls but still finished on the losing side against Lancashire in 1995.

1998 Benson and Hedges Cup final at Lord's.

BENSON AND HEDGES CUP PERFORMANCES

The oddest Gold Award was probably made after the 1984 final when Lancashire beat Warwickshire by six wickets.

Essex beat Leicestershire, Benson and Hedges Cup 1998.

THE adjudicator that day, Peter May, gave the award to the winning captain John Abrahams, who didn't bowl and was out for a duck when he batted. However, he did field with enthusiasm and led his team well.

There have been a number of giant-killing performances in the competition, the Combined Universities and Minor Counties recording several victories over first-class counties. Two of the most notable wins were Scotland's victory over Northamptonshire at Northampton in 1990 and Ireland's win in 1997 against a Middlesex side captained by Mike Gatting by 46 runs at Castle Avenue, Dublin.

However, Ireland have also been on the receiving end of two of the biggest defeats recorded in the competition. They lost to Somerset by 233 runs at Eglinton in 1995 and two years later lost heavily again to Somerset, by 221 runs at Taunton – four days after their famous triumph over Middlesex.

Glamorgan's Malcolm Nash hit the fastest century when he reached three figures in 62 minutes against Hampshire at Swansea in 1976. There have been some excellent performances with the ball over the years, with Shaun Pollock leading the way. The South African Test all-rounder took four wickets in four balls when playing for Warwickshire against Leicestershire at Edgbaston in 1996.

The last Benson and Hedges Cup final.

Benson and Hedges
Cup Winners

1972	Leicestershire – beat Yorkshire by five wickets
1973	Kent – beat Worcestershire by 39 runs
1974	Surrey – beat Leicestershire by 27 runs
1975	Leicestershire – beat Middlesex by five wickets
1976	Kent – beat Worcestershire by 43 runs
1977	Gloucestershire – beat Kent by 64 runs
1978	Kent – beat Derbyshire by six wickets
1979	Essex – beat Surrey by 35 runs
1980	Northamptonshire – beat Essex by six runs
1981	Somerset – beat Surrey by seven wickets
1982	Somerset – beat Nottinghamshire by nine wickets
1983	Middlesex – beat Essex by four runs
1984	Lancashire – beat Warwickshire by six wickets
1985	Leicestershire – beat Essex by five wickets
1986	Middlesex – beat Kent by two runs
1987	Yorkshire – beat Northamptonshire having taken more wickets after the scores finished level

1988	Hampshire – beat Derbyshire by seven wickets
1989	Nottinghamshire – beat Essex by three wickets
1990	Lancashire – beat Worcestershire by 69 runs
1991	Worcestershire – beat Lancashire by 65 runs
1992	Hampshire – beat Kent by 41 runs
1993	Derbyshire – beat Lancashire by six runs
1994	Warwickshire – beat Worcestershire by six wickets
1995	Lancashire – beat Kent by 35 runs
1996	Lancashire – beat Northamptonshire by 31 runs
1997	Surrey – beat Kent by eight wickets
1998	Essex – beat Leicestershire by 192 runs

1998 Final at Lord's; 11 and 12 June

Essex 268-7 (50 overs. Prichard 92, Hussain 88). Leicestershire 76 (27.4 overs). Essex won by 192 runs. Gold Award: P. J. Prichard.

Essex triumph at Lord's in 1998.

Minor Counties League

The Minor Counties Cricket Association was formed in 1895 and immediately set up the Minor Counties Championship. Seven sides competed in the first season: Bedfordshire, Durham, Hertfordshire, Norfolk, Oxfordshire, Staffordshire and Worcestershire. The first Championship title was shared by Durham, Norfolk and Worcestershire.

UNTIL FAIRLY RECENTLY a number of first-class counties entered their second-eleven teams in the Minor Counties Championship in a policy designed to give emerging young players a chance to face strong opposition. The last county second-eleven to win the title was Yorkshire II in 1971. In recent years the first-class counties have competed in their own second-eleven competitions.

Relations between the Minor Counties have not always been cordial; at one time there appeared to be a north–south divide in terms of policy. Clubs from the north were run on a semi-professional basis, while counties further South seemed to prefer a more 'amateur' style of approach. Things have changed considerably now as Devon's amazing run of success proves.

A number of former first-class players turn out for their adopted Minor Counties and add much interest for the crowds and boost media coverage. Former England Test batsmen Derek Randall and Wayne Larkins have scored many runs for Suffolk and Bedfordshire respectively. Former Kent and Leicestershire all-rounder Laurie Potter is still a key player for champions Staffordshire.

Before first-class counties were allowed to sign overseas

players, Minor Counties matches were graced with some great Test stars; often a Minor Counties batsman would suddenly find himself about to face an emerging West Indies' fast bowling star of the future.

MINOR COUNTIES LEAGUE TODAY

In recent years, Devon and Staffordshire have been the two dominant sides at this level. Devon, captained by former Somerset player Peter Roebuck, captured their seventh trophy in seven years when they beat Shropshire by eight wickets in the 1998 MCC Trophy Final at Lord's on 26 August.

THE DEVONIANS WON the Minor Counties Championship for an unprecedented four consecutive seasons between 1994 and 1997, as well as claiming the MCC Trophy again in 1992 and 1994. Many critics rate Devon's Nick Folland as currently the best batsman outside the County Championship in England.

In 1998 the Minor Counties agreed to a request from the England and Wales Cricket Board (ECB) to play a certain number of matches using the Australian 'grade' model: one-innings matches being played over two days. Staffordshire, who were not keen initially on these experimental matches, nevertheless performed strongly over the season, and went on to win the Championship when they finally managed to dislodge Devon from the top of the table. Staffordshire, captained by the impressive Steve Dean, have now won the Championship on a record ten occasions.

overleaf: Durham County Cricket Club

BROWN ALE

Championship Winners
Since the Second World War

1946	Suffolk	**1973**	Shropshire
1947	Yorkshire II	**1974**	Oxfordshire
1948	Lancashire II	**1975**	Hertfordshire
1949	Lancashire II	**1976**	Durham
1950	Surrey II	**1977**	Suffolk
1951	Kent II	**1978**	Devon
1952	Buckinghamshire	**1979**	Suffolk
1953	Berkshire	**1980**	Durham
1954	Surrey II	**1981**	Durham
1955	Surrey II	**1982**	Oxfordshire
1956	Kent II	**1983**	Hertfordshire
1957	Yorkshire II	**1984**	Durham
1958	Yorkshire II	**1985**	Cheshire
1959	Warwickshire II	**1986**	Cumberland
1960	Lancashire II	**1987**	Buckinghamshire
1961	Somerset II	**1988**	Cheshire
1962	Warwickshire II	**1989**	Oxfordshire
1963	Cambridgeshire	**1990**	Hertfordshire
1964	Lancashire II	**1991**	Staffordshire
1965	Somerset II	**1992**	Staffordshire
1966	Lincolnshire	**1993**	Staffordshire
1967	Cheshire	**1994**	Devon
1968	Yorkshire II	**1995**	Devon
1969	Buckinghamshire	**1996**	Devon
1970	Bedfordshire	**1997**	Devon
1971	Yorkshire II	**1998**	Staffordshire
1972	Bedfordshire		

1998 Championship Play-off Final
at Dean Park, Bournemouth; 6 and 7 September
Staffordshire 171-6 (50 overs. Potter 58) & 170-9
(68.1 overs. Dean 59, Potter 52, Cowley 7 for 55).
Dorset 92 (37.5 overs. Potter 4 for 6, Richardson 4
for 29). Staffordshire won on superior run-rate

MCC Trophy Winners

1983	Cheshire
1984	Hertfordshire
1985	Durham
1986	Norfolk
1987	Cheshire
1988	Dorset
1989	Cumberland
1990	Buckinghamshire
1991	Staffordshire
1992	Devon
1993	Staffordshire
1994	Devon
1995	Cambridgeshire
1996	Cheshire
1997	Norfolk
1998	Devon

1998 MCC Trophy Final at Lord's;
26 August. Shropshire 201-9 (60 overs).
Devon 204-2 (41.5 overs. Folland 77no,
Pugh 71no). Devon won by eight wickets.

INTERNATIONAL CRICKET
Introduction

With nine countries currently full members of the ICC it is likely that at any time during the year, a Test series will be underway somewhere. Keen public interest in one-day internationals has also seen the limited-overs version of the game develop at a tremendous pace.

INNOVATIONS SUCH AS coloured strips for the players and the introduction of floodlights for day/night for one-day matches have helped make cricket a spectacle not just for those at the ground but also for a booming television audience.

There have been many changes in world cricket over the past twenty years or so and no doubt there are more to come.

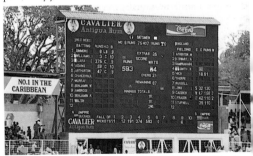

West Indies v England in Antigua, 1994 – a historic score for Brian Lara.

England v Sri Lanka at the Oval, 1998.

INTERNATIONAL CRICKET TODAY

ENGLAND'S EARLY dominance of international cricket was challenged, initially by Australia, and as more countries began playing at the highest level, teams such as South Africa and the West Indies started to offer competitive opposition, too.

Sri Lanka's victory over Australia in the Wills World Cup Final in Lahore in March 1996 confirmed that country's progress as a force in international cricket. They demonstrated clearly that they are by no means just a one-day team by comprehensively beating England in a one-off Test at The Oval in August 1998.

In recent years Pakistan, South Africa and Australia have all claimed to be the best Test side in the world but without ratification by the ICC. There have been calls for an official Test match world championship and no doubt it will happen in some shape or form.

Australia

> There is surprisingly little first-class cricket played in Australia compared to England. The Sheffield Shield competition comprises of just six state sides: New South Wales, Queensland, South Australia, Tasmania, Victoria and Western Australia.

THE TEAMS PLAY each other twice and apart from Test matches and state matches against touring sides, an Australian cricketer plays a maximum of just ten first-class matches per season. New South Wales have been the strongest state side over the years since the Sheffield Shield was introduced in 1892–93 and have won the title 45 times out of a possible 95.

Australia play a good standard of club cricket (known as grade cricket) and some argue this helps develop young players more successfully than pitching them into a never-ending round of County Championship matches as often happens in England.

Australia v England, 1983.

New Zealand

First-class cricket in New Zealand received a boost in 1975 when Shell Oil agreed a lucrative sponsorship package.

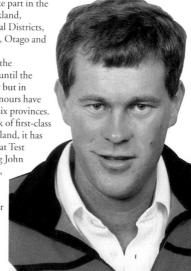

AS A RESULT OF the deal, the Plunket Shield – the country's major domestic competition – was renamed the Shell Trophy and the first-class game in general became better organised. Six provincial sides take part in the Shell Trophy: Auckland, Canterbury, Central Districts, Northern Districts, Otago and Wellington.

Auckland were the strongest province until the Second World War but in recent years the honours have been shared by all six provinces.

Despite the lack of first-class cricket in New Zealand, it has produced some great Test cricketers including John Reid, Bert Sutcliffe, Glenn Turner and, more recently, that great all-rounder Sir Richard Hadlee.

John Reid of New Zealand.

South Africa

South Africa's main first-class competition is the Supersport Series. It was originally the Currie Cup when it was introduced in 1889–90 and renamed the Castle Cup between 1990–91 and 1995–96.

NINE TEAMS CURRENTLY compete in the tournament: Boland, Border, Eastern Province, Free State, Griqualand West, Natal, Northerns, Gauteng and Western Province.

South Africa were banned from playing international cricket because of its government's apartheid policy and throughout the 1970s and 1980s, apart from so-called 'rebel' tours, no competitive matches were played against foreign opposition. South Africa had potentially the best side in the world in the early 1970s, but players such as Graeme Pollock, Eddie Barlow, Mike Procter and Barry Richards were lost to the world stage. South Africa was allowed back into Test cricket in 1991–92.

The United Cricket Board of South Africa has made changes to the Supersport Series, the first of which came into effect for the 1998–99 series. It is hoped that this restructuring will strengthen the player base there.

Graeme Pollock of South Africa.

Zimbabwe

Zimbabwe are the youngest of the Test-playing nations, having been granted full membership of the ICC in July 1992.

Andy Flower (left) and Grant Flower (right) of Zimbabwe.

HOWEVER, THERE has been a strong cricket tradition in the country – formerly known as Rhodesia – that dates back to the nineteenth century. For many years Rhodesia played as a team in neighbouring South Africa's Currie Cup.

Matches in Zimbabwe were not given first-class status until as recently as 1993–94 when four teams (Mashonaland, Mashonaland Country Districts, Mashonaland Under-24s and Matabeleland) competed for the Logan Trophy. In the 1996–97 the Zimbabwean cricketing authorities decided to reduce the number of competing teams to just two (Mashonaland and Matabeleland) and the competition was decided over a best-of-three series which Mashonaland won 2–0.

West Indies

Transportation difficulties before the introduction of air travel hindered the development of a major domestic competition in the West Indies.

IT WAS NOT UNTIL 1965–66 that the first sponsored regional tournament, the Shell Shield, was inaugurated. The tournament became the Red Stripe Cup in 1987–88.

Six teams (Barbados, Guyana, Jamaica, the Leeward Islands, Trinidad & Tobago and the Windward Islands) take part and played each just once until 1996–97 when the West Indies Cricket Board decided that matches should be played on a home and away basis in an effort to provide more first-class competition to help develop young talent.

Barbados – home of Sir Garfield Sobers – has been the strongest team, claiming the title 14 times in 31 years. There was no competition in 1967–68.

Curtly Ambrose of the West Indies.

Sri Lanka

Sri Lanka surprised much of the cricketing world with their carefree approach to the one-day game, but it was a tactic that saw them win the 1996 World Cup and continue to do well against all opposition in limited-overs internationals.

THEY have not been as successful in Tests however, although their demolition of England by nine wickets at The Oval in August 1998 suggests they are finding their feet at this level.

The major domestic competition is now known as the P. Saravanamuttu ('Sara') Trophy and has been contested since 1988–89. 14 sides compete in the tournament, which was known as the Lakspray Trophy for the first two years of its existence. Prior to its introduction the only matches given first-class status in Sri Lanka were those played against touring parties.

Aravinda de Silva of Sri Lanka.

India

The dry, slow wickets in India have helped produce many world-class batsmen with excellent technique and limitless patience.

THE NAMES OF K. S. Ranjitsinhji, who subsequently played for England, Cambridge University and Sussex, the Nawab of Pataudi, Sunil Gavaskar and, more recently, Sachin Tendulkar spring to mind.

The Ranji Trophy was named after the great Ranjitsinhji. Since 1946 – when the Bombay Pentagular tournament was scrapped – the Ranji Trophy has been the premier domestic competition in India. Mumbai, formerly known as Bombay, have won the trophy 33 times in 63 years since its inception in 1934–35.

The Duleep Trophy – named after Ranjitsinhji's nephew K. S. Duleepsinhji – is also held. It is an inter-zonal tournament played on a knock-out basis and was introduced in 1961–62.

Sachin Tendulkar of India.

Pakistan

Pakistan quickly proved to be a force in world cricket after being granted full Test status in 1952 following its partition from India in 1947.

WITHIN THE SPACE of just seven years they had beaten Australia, New Zealand and the West Indies in Test rubbers and recorded victories over England and India.

There are two main domestic competitions in Pakistan: the Qaid-E-Azam Trophy, the premier national championship – inaugurated in 1953–54 and dominated by Karachi Blues, Karachi Whites and Lahore City in recent years – and the PCB Patron's Trophy, introduced in 1960–61. The PCB has also been called the Ayub Trophy and the BCCP Trophy. Between 1979–80 and 1982–83 it was used as a qualifying contest for the Qaid-E-Azam Trophy and the matches were not considered first-class.

Hanif Mohammed of Pakistan.

INTERNATIONAL COMPETITIONS
Test Matches

Test match cricket has always been by far and away the most rewarding version of the game for both player and cricketing aficionado. Played at its best there is no better spectacle in sport.

MANY GREAT STARS over the years have graced cricket fields throughout the world in Test matches and have brought delight and pleasure to millions.

An ecstatic home crowd after England win the Ashes, 1981.

Who could ever forget having seen Sir Donald Bradman, Walter Hammond and Sir Jack Hobbs display the art of batsmanship or Harold Larwood and Sydney Barnes demonstrate the skills of fast and swing bowling respectively. Or the sight of Sir Gary Sobers elegantly stroking the ball to the boundary or bemusing a batsman with his various bowling techniques? In modern times a number of fast bowlers have bowled like demons – such as Australia's Dennis Lillee and Jeff Thomson and the West Indies' Michael Holding and Malcolm Marshall. Plus of course, cricket fans have been lucky enough to

England v Australia at the Oval, 1948.

see genuinely great all-rounders in the shape of England's Ian Botham and Pakistan's Imran Khan – not forgetting New Zealand's Sir Richard Hadlee and India's Kapil Dev. All have been great players and all have performed to the best of their ability at the highest level – Test match cricket.

One-day internationals, with all their innovations such as coloured kits for the players and day/night matches played under floodlights, are certainly exciting affairs. They are equally appealing to the spectator, sponsor and broadcaster. The revenue they bring into cricket is vital and without it the sport would undoubtedly struggle to survive in its present form.

EARLY TEST MATCHES

Every young player has the ambition to represent their country at Test level and the five-day version of cricket remains the sport's purest form.

THE EARLY TUSSLES between England and Australia, the two early powers of world cricket, set the tone for Test match cricket. The matches were played with aggression but by men who had the cricketing skills to complement their will to win.

THE ASHES

THE SUCCESS of the early combative Tests between England and Australia caught the public's imagination and the introduction of 'the Ashes' as the prize for winning a Test series between the old enemies proves the point. When Australia inflicted England's first defeat on home soil *The Sporting Times* published a mock obituary. It read: 'In affectionate remembrance of English cricket which died at The Oval on 29 August 1882. Deeply lamented by a large circle of sorrowing friends and acquaintants – RIP. Note: The body will be cremated and the ashes taken to Australia.'

In Affectionate Remembrance
OF
ENGLISH CRICKET,
WHICH DIED AT THE OVAL
ON
29th AUGUST, 1882,
Deeply lamented by a large circle of sorrowing friends and acquaintances.

R.I.P.

N.B.—*The body will be cremated and the ashes taken to Australia.*

The origin of the Ashes, 1882.

During England's tour of Australia later that year a social match was played at the estate of Sir William Clarke and Lady Clarke. After the game had finished Lady Clarke burnt a bail and placed the ashes in a small wooden urn. She then presented it to the England captain, the Hon. Ivo Bligh, Earl of Darnley. The urn was kept by Bligh at his Cobham Hall estate until his death in 1927, whereupon his widow sent it to Lord's for safekeeping. It is housed in the Memorial Gallery at Lord's and never removed, even when Australia have won a series and 'hold' the Ashes. Australia have had the beating of England in recent years and between 1989 and 1997 won five consecutive series. The 1997 Australian party had the courage to ask Lord's if they could take the Ashes back home with them – their request was politely but firmly turned down.

A replica of the Ashes urn.

CONTROVERSIAL TEST MATCHES

The Tests played in Australia on England's tour of 1932–33 were perhaps the most controversial. England's captain Douglas Jardine ordered his fast bowlers Harold Larwood and Bill Voce to pitch the ball short at the bodies of the Australian batsmen.

A LINE OF ENGLISH fielders were placed close in on the leg side to snap up any catches off the bat or gloves. After a number of Australian batsmen received painful knocks on the head and upper body several angry cables flew between Australia and Lord's and at one stage it looked as if the series would be called off. It survived and went down in history as the infamous 'Bodyline' series.

There was further tension on England's 1958–59 tour of Australia when the tourists thought some of the Australian bowlers were throwing the ball.

On England's

1970–71 tour, their fast bowler John Snow's use of the short-pitched delivery upset certain sections of the crowd and several spectators threatened at one stage to take action of their own against the Sussex player. Thankfully, common sense prevailed in the end.

Douglas Jardine (right) greets Larwood and Voce, 1932.

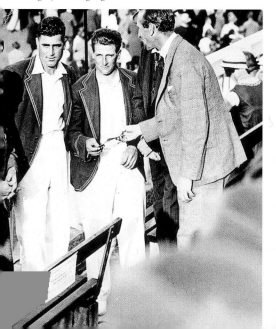

NEW TEST CONTENDERS

The emergence of other Test match-playing countries offered a different challenge to the old powers, England and Australia. The emergence of South Africa in the early 1900s provided England with another touring opportunity.

INDIA, THE West Indies and New Zealand became Test match-playing countries in 1926 and added further dimensions in terms of local climate and playing conditions.

The rapid development of air travel meant that overseas tours were easier to plan and more comfortable for the players. As a result more and more Test matches were played, with new Test stars emerging all the time.

England v South Africa, 1998.

'Botham's Test': England v Australia, 1981.

TESTS AND TELEVISION

TODAY'S TEST MATCHES receive excellent live television coverage throughout the world. Because of satellite and cable transmission, the cricket fan can watch practically every ball bowled in a Test match involving England in any country in the world. Every delivery, shot, catch or stop in the field is analysed in detail by the pundits.

The television cameras have recorded for posterity some of the greatest moments in Test match history. Anyone who watched the 1981 Headingley Test match between England and Australia will never forget 'Botham's Test'. News of England's amazing recovery led by the Somerset all-rounder even stopped proceedings in the House of Commons as MPs were advised of the latest score.

Test Records

HIGHEST INDIVIDUAL INNINGS

375	*B. C. Lara* West Indies v England at St John's 1993–94	
365*	*G. S. Sobers* West Indies v Pakistan at Kingston 1957–58	
364	*L. Hutton* England v Australia at The Oval 1938	
340	*S. T. Jayasuriya* Sri Lanka v India at Colombo 1997–98	
337	*Hanif Mohammed* Pakistan v West Indies at Bridgetown 1957–58	
336*	*W. R. Hammond* England v New Zealand at Auckland 1932–33	
334	*D. G. Bradman* Australia v England at Headingley 1930	
333	*G. A. Gooch* England v India at Lord's 1990	
325	*A. Sandham* England v West Indies at Kingston 1929–30	
311	*R. B. Simpson* Australia v England at Old Trafford 1964	

* Not out

MOST RUNS IN TEST CAREER

11,174 *A. R. Border* (Australia) Tests 156 Innings 265 Ave 50.56

10,122 *S. M. Gavaskar* (India) Tests 125 Innings 214 Ave 51.12

8,900 *G. A. Gooch* (England) Tests 118 Innings 215 Ave 42.58

8,832 *Javed Miandad* (Pakistan) Tests 124 Innings 189 Ave 52.57

8,540 *I. V. A. Richards* (West Indies) Tests 121 Innings 182 Ave 50.23

8,231 *D. I. Gower* (England) Tests 117 Innings 204 Ave 44.25

8,114 *G. Boycott* (England) Tests 108 Innings 193 Ave 47.72

8,032 *G. S. Sobers* (West Indies) Tests 93 Innings 160 Ave 57.78

7,624 *M. C. Cowdrey* (Eng.) Tests 114 Innings 188 Ave 44.06

7,558 *C. G. Greenidge* (West Indies) Tests 108 Innings 185 Ave 44.72

OTHER RECORDS

AUSTRALIA'S Sir Donald Bradman has recorded the highest average in a Test career. He played in only 52 Tests and in 80 innings scored 6,996 runs for an average of 99.94. Had Bradman scored four in his final innings he would have finished with an average of 100, but he was bowled second ball for nought. He hit 29 Test centuries, with a highest score of 334.

Viv Richards hit the fastest Test century in terms of balls faced when he reached three figures off just 56 balls when playing for West Indies against England at St John's in 1985–86.

Viv Richards

Bowling Records

MOST WICKETS IN A CAREER

434	*Kapil Dev* (India) Tests 131 Runs 12,867 Ave 29.64	
431	*R. J. Hadlee* (New Zealand) Tests 86 Runs 9,612 Ave 22.29	
383	*I. T. Botham* (England) Tests 102 Runs 10,878 Ave 28.40	
376	*M. D. Marshall* (West Indies) Tests 81 Runs 7,876 Ave 20.94	
375	*C. A. Walsh* (West Indies) Tests 93 Runs 8,789 Ave 25.95	
362	*Imran Khan* (Pakistan) Tests 88 Runs 8,258 Ave 22.81	
355	*D. K. Lillee* (Australia) Tests 70 Runs 8,493 Ave 23.92	
341	*Wasim Akram* (Pakistan) Tests 94 Runs 7,705 Ave 22.59	
337	*C. E. L. Ambrose* (West Indies) Tests 90 Runs 7,133 Ave 21.16	
325	*R. G. D. Willis* (England) Tests 90 Runs 8,190 Ave 25.20	

TOP THREE BOWLING ANALYSES

J. C. Laker

(England) 51.2-23-53-10, against Australia
at Old Trafford in 1956

G. A. Lohmann

(England) 14.2-6-28-9 against South Africa
at Johannesburg in 1895–96

J. C. Laker

(England) 16.4-4-37-9, against Australia
at Old Trafford in 1956

- Jim Laker's match return of 19 for 90 against Australia remains the best in Test, and first-class, cricket.

Kapil Dev, who has taken most wickets in his career.

OTHER RECORDS

ON 3 OCTOBER 1998 in the First Test at Rawalpindi
between Pakistan and Australia, wicket-keeper Ian Healy broke
the world record of compatriot Rodney Marsh when he
claimed his 356th Test match victim – caught Wasim Akram
off the bowling of off-spinner Colin Miller. His total was made
up of 331 catches and 25 stumpings spread over 104 Tests.

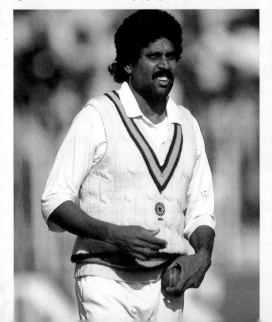

One-day Internationals

International one-day cricket started almost
by accident. Rain had totally devastated the first four
days of a scheduled Test match between Australia
and England at Melbourne. To satisfy a disappointed
crowd, the two teams decided to abandon the Test
and play a one-day, limited-overs match instead
on 5 January 1971.

IT WAS IRONIC that the match was played on the ground
where Test cricket started 94 years earlier and, as in the
match back in 1877, Australia were the victors. The response
from the Australian public was astonishing and shocked the
cricket establishment worldwide. The match attracted 46,000
spectators and from that moment international cricket would
never be the same again.

Australia's Graeme McKenzie bowled the first ball in one-
day internationals to Geoff Boycott. His team-mate Jeff
Thomson took the first wicket when he had Boycott caught by
Bill Lawry. England's John Edrich reached the first half-century
in these matches and went on to make 82 and claim the Man
of the Match award.

As a result of the public's response to the game, Australia's
schedule for their tour of England the following summer was
rearranged, with the sixth Test being replaced by three limited-
overs matches.

Dennis Amiss went down in the record books as the first
player to score a century in these matches when he reached that
milestone against Australia at Old Trafford on 24 August 1972.

So great was the appetite for this form of cricket that just four years after that historic one-day encounter in Melbourne, the inaugural World Cup was staged in England.

Australia v the World Supertest, Sydney 1979.

'THE PACKER CIRCUS'

Kerry Packer, the Australian tycoon, then entered the picture and changed the face of cricket forever.

WHEN HIS APPROACH for broadcasting rights was turned down by the Australian Cricket Board, he decided to bankroll his own competition instead. He signed up more than 40 of the world's top players and after ultimate success in the law courts, World Series Cricket was launched.

'The Packer Circus', as it was universally referred to, introduced day/night matches under floodlights and coloured clothing for players. It also featured enhanced camera work during broadcasts. Cricket's establishment took Packer on and lost, but it can be argued that the long-term benefits to cricket, especially the improved financial rewards for the players, far outweigh any disadvantages. Money has come into the sport as a direct result of Packer's interest, and cash-strapped Test cricket – a moribund beast that was dying a slow, agonising death – has certainly benefited. Not only has the revenue helped save Test cricket, but the standard of play and fitness has improved – especially the fielding.

All of Packer's so-called rebels were available again for their official national squads for the 1979 World Cup – which was again held in England and retained by a brilliant West Indies team, captained by Clive Lloyd and featuring the masterful Viv Richards and a battery of superb fast bowlers. The West Indies and Australia continued to dominate one-day internationals and it was a surprise when India beat Lloyd's team to win the third World Cup at Lord's in 1983.

Packer cricket – Sydney, 1979.

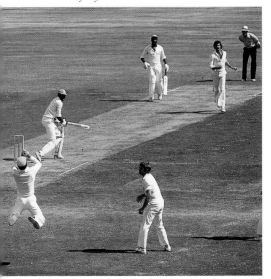

ONE-DAY CHAMPIONS

India and their neighbours Pakistan, together with a Richard Hadlee-inspired New Zealand, began to beat the West Indies and Australia on a regular basis. England faced the same fate and suddenly there were no weak countries playing one-day internationals.

England v New Zealand, 3rd test 1990: Richard Hadlee (NZ).

JUST AS THE cricketing nations of the world were cancelling each other out with tried and tested one-day tactics along came Sri Lanka, who proceeded to throw the coaching manual out of the window. Their marvellous, wristy batsmen started to play their shots from the first ball of an innings – taking advantage of the restrictions placed on the fielding captain, who can only have two fieldsmen outside an arc drawn 30 yards from each wicket for the first 15 overs and five for the rest of the innings. This prevents negative captains from positioning all the fieldsmen on the boundary. However, Sri Lanka kept hitting boundaries even after the field could be spread far and wide. The Sri Lankans took the 1996 World Cup by storm and easily beat a perplexed Australian side in the final in Lahore.

With South Africa's welcomed return to international cricket and Zimbabwe's emergence onto the world stage, there are now more than enough countries ready and willing to keep the seemingly endless schedule of one-day international series buzzing.

India v Sri Lanka, 1996: Aravinda de Silva (Sri Lanka).

Record Holders

Note: One of the problems with publishing any kind of statistics associated with cricket is that they can be, and usually are, out of date before the ink has dried or the cricket buff has pressed his 'store' button on his personal computer. Because there are so many one-day internationals played nowadays records can tumble on a regular basis.

BATTING

Highest individual scores

194	*Saeed Anwar* Pakistan v India at Chennai in 1996–97
189*	*I. V. A. Richards* West Indies v England at Old Trafford in 1984
188*	*G. Kirsten* South Africa v UAE at Rawalpindi in 1995–96
181	*I. V. A. Richards* West Indies v Sri Lanka at Karachi in 1987–88
175*	*Kapil Dev* India v Zimbabwe Tunbridge Wells in 1983
171*	*G. M. Turner* New Zealand v East Africa at Edgbaston in 1975
169*	*D. J. Callaghan* South Africa v New Zealand at Verwoerdburg in 1994–95
169	*B. C. Lara* West Indies v Sri Lanka at Sharjah in 1995–96

- The highest individual score by an English batsman is the 167* made by Hampshire's Robin Smith against Australia at Edgbaston in 1993.

* **Not out**

Leading wicket takers

333 *Wasim Akram* (Pakistan) Matches 232 Runs 7,517
Ave 22.57

265 *Waqar Younis* (Pakistan) Matches 156 Runs 5,762
Ave 21.74

253 *Kapil Dev* (India) Matches 224 Runs 6,945
Ave 27.45

203 *C. J. McDermott* (Australia) Matches 138 Runs 5,018
Ave 24.71

200 *C. E. L. Ambrose* (West Indies) Matches 146 Runs 4,518
Ave 22.59

196 *C. A. Walsh* (West Indies) Matches 176 Runs 5,936
Ave 30.28

182 *Imran Khan* (Pakistan) Matches 175 Runs 4,845
Ave 26.62

182 *S. R. Waugh* (Australia) Matches 221 Runs 5,877
Ave 34.16

- Pakistan's Aqib Javed returned the best bowling analysis – 7 for 37 – against India at Sharjah in 1991–92.
- The best bowling analysis by an England bowler remains Vic Marks' 5 for 20 against New Zealand at Wellington in 1983–84.

MOST RUNS

8,648 *D. L. Haynes* (West Indies) Matches 238 Innings 237
Ave 41.37

7,382 *Javed Miandad* (Pakistan) Matches 233 Innings 218
Ave 41.70

7,294 *M. Azharuddin* (India) Matches 259 Innings 239
Ave 37.79

6,884 *Salim Malik* (Pakistan) Matches 268 Innings 242
Ave 33.58

6,874 *P. A. de Silva* (Sri Lanka) Matches 218 Innings 212
Ave 36.17

6,721 *I. V. A. Richards* (West Indies) Matches 187 Innings 167
Ave 47.00

6,524 *A. R. Border* (Australia) Matches 273 Innings 252
Ave 30.62

6,249 *R. B. Richardson* (West Indies) Matches 224 Innings 217
Ave 33.41

- Sri Lanka recorded the highest total in limited-overs internationals when they made 398-5 off 50 overs against Kenya at Kandy in 1995–96.
- England's highest total is 363-7, made off 55 overs, against Pakistan at Trent Bridge in 1992.
- Pakistan made the lowest score – 43 all out against West Indies at Cape Town in 1992–93.

West Indies' Haynes retains the record for the highest ever total of runs

International Tours

The so-called 'Packer Revolution' of the
1970s was not the only example of a rebellion
upsetting the plans of cricket's administrators.
The first planned overseas tour was organised
by the Duke of Dorset, Britain's Ambassador
to France – a cricket enthusiast and keen
patron of the game, who invited an England
side to Paris in August 1789.

JUST AS THE England party was about to set out on
their trip across the Channel, the French Revolution
broke out and the tour was quickly abandoned when the
team, having arrived at Dover to board their ship, saw the
Duke of Dorset fleeing back to England to escape the
turmoil in Paris.

Fred Lillywhite organised the first touring party that
actually left England. The team was captained by George
Parr and visited Canada and the United States. The party left
Liverpool on 7 September 1859 and did not arrive in
Quebec until 22 September. The players had to endure a
series of hardships, not least icebergs and storms. The
tourists won all their five matches and returned home on
11 November, having travelled an estimated 7,500 miles in
two months.

The first overseas tour to visit England was made by a
team of Australian Aborigines in 1868 just four years after
overarm bowling had been made legal. That historic first tour
was commemorated in 1988 by a visit by the newly-formed
Aborigine Cricket Association.

Australia meets the English eleven at Sheffield Park, Sussex, in 1896.

EARLY TOURS

Britain continued to build its empire during the second half of the nineteenth century and soldiers and sailors began playing impromptu matches against local teams in various parts of the world.

THE SPORT OF cricket was being introduced in many countries and there was a growing desire to play against overseas opposition. The problem was that overseas travel was still difficult and at times downright dangerous. The party that toured North America nearly experienced the same fate in the Atlantic as the *Titanic*, and the threat of seasickness and other more serious ailments, did not encourage the would-be travelling cricketer.

However, tours to and from Australia became regular occurrences, and South Africa was added to the itinerary as it became the third Test-playing nation. The West Indies, India and New Zealand also became regular destinations from the 1920s as they too started playing Test matches and long-distance travel began to improve.

Sir Garfield Sobers of the West Indies, 1957.

After the Second World War, when long-haul flying became the normal mode of transport, tours became more popular and itineraries less exhausting for the players. Modern aviation now allows a team to be jetted to all parts of the world in comfort.

England v South Africa: the first first-class match played in Soweto, 1995.

INTERNATIONAL TOURS TODAY

It is often said that a tour party plays better as a team than the hosts. It can be argued that a group of 16 or 17 players together for anything up to three months or more pull together in adversity.

THE TOURING PARTY'S selection committee has fewer players to pick from and that can sometimes help form a cohesive and rigid policy. The home selectors in any country have a tendency to panic if their team is doing badly and, under pressure from the media, can make the oddest choices.

The Australian tourists are rumoured to start their bonding on the flight to Heathrow. Over the years they have allegedly had a contest involving cans of lager. The winner is the player who has managed to drink the most 'tinnies' before the aeroplane reaches London. Once they have landed, they insist the job in hand – that of winning the Ashes series – is well and truly focused upon.

Modern cricket is all about fitness and health, and if the Aussies do have their drinking contest on the way over, the team doctor and physio will certainly keep them in check for the rest of the tour.

England have experienced some troubles on tour in recent years, and stories of alleged misdemeanours have appeared in the news sections of the tabloids. On one recent tour of Australia, there were rumoured to be more gossip column journalists than cricket writers following the England party.

International tours have certainly changed since the days when a team watched all its gear put on to a steam ship, embarked and then had to wait weeks before they could play cricket on *terra firma*.

England training in Lanzarote, 1997.

THE WORLD CUP

> The public interest in one-day cricket, together with the
> fact that broadcasters found the limited-overs package
> highly attractive, led to the ICC backing the idea of a
> World Cup tournament similar to that contested by other
> sports such as soccer. There would be group qualifying
> matches followed by a knock-out stage leading to a final.

1975

THE FIRST World Cup was contested in 1975 with England as the host country. The tournament was blessed with excellent weather throughout and proved to be a great success.

The final at Lord's was a classic confrontation between the West Indies and Australia, whose captain Ian Chappell won the toss and put the opposition in. Skipper Clive Lloyd made a brilliant 102 and former captain Rohan Kanhai chipped in with 55 as the West Indies made 291 for 8 off their allotted 60 overs.

Australia made steady progress as they chased their target, with skipper Chappell making 62. But they kept losing wickets and when the ninth wicket fell at 233, the match looked to be all but over. However, the last wicket pair Jeff Thomson and Dennis Lillee then edged their team closer and closer to the West Indies total before Thomson became the fifth Australian to be run out in the innings – and the West Indies won the match by 17 runs.

World Cup final 1975: West Indies captain Clive Lloyd during his 100.

1983

THE THIRD WORLD Cup was also played in England and this time an over-confident West Indies side were surprisingly beaten in a low-scoring final by the underdogs India.

1987

THE 1987 event was hosted jointly by India and Pakistan and the number of overs per side reduced to 50. The final saw Australia face England in Calcutta. Australia made 253 for 5 off their allotted overs, with opener David Boon making 75. England appeared to be cruising to victory before skipper Mike Gatting attempted a reverse sweep against Australian captain Allan Border and was caught. England never recovered to keep up with the required run-rate and lost a close match by 7 runs.

World Cup final 1987: Gatting is caught.

1992

THE 1992 WORLD Cup, the first to employ coloured clothing, a white ball and floodlights, was staged in Australia and New Zealand and again England reached the final in Melbourne. Their opponents were Pakistan, who made 249 for 6 off 50 overs, with captain Imran Khan making 72 and Javed Miandad 58. Although one-day specialist Neil Fairbrother made 62, England never really looked like overhauling Pakistan's total and lost by 22 runs.

World Cup final 1992: Imran Khan lifts the trophy.

1996

THE 1996 TOURNAMENT was again hosted jointly by India and Pakistan and this time it was the underrated Sri Lanka side that took the competition by storm. They brought a new approach to the one-day game and one of their tactics was to exploit the restrictions on the fielding side in the first 15 overs of an innings. The fielding captain is limited to the number of players he can position in the

World Cup 1996: Paul Adams of Pakistan

deep at the start of an innings and the Sri Lankans took full advantage by going for the runs at beginning of their 50 overs, rather than waiting to slog at every ball in the last 10 overs.

The Sri Lankans' aggressive approach to the early stages of their innings was copied around the world – even in the English county one-day game, where many teams sent in an attacking lower order batsman to open the innings. This player is known as a 'pinch-hitter', a phrase borrowed from baseball in America. He is a sacrifice – a batter who will score runs quickly if he stays, but will not be a major loss if he is out cheaply.

Arjuna Ranatunga, the Sri Lanka skipper, won the toss and invited Australia to bat, a bold move as no team batting second had won in the previous five World Cup finals.

Mark Taylor scored 74 off 83 balls as the Australians got off to good start and with Rick Ponting added 101 for the second wicket. At this stage the Sri Lankans were facing a considerable total. However, Ranatunga then used his slower bowlers for the rest of the innings and restricted Australia to a rather disappointing 241.

Sri Lanka made a shaky start to their innings and lost both openers for just 23 runs. However, Aravinda de Silva then took control of the situation. He put on 125 with Gurusinha, who made 65, for the third wicket and then shared an unbroken fourth wicket stand of 97 with skipper Ranatunga, who made 47 not out.

De Silva, who was named Man of the Match, was undefeated on 107 at the end as Sri Lanka reached their target with 3.4 overs remaining.

England will again host the World Cup in 1999.

Aravinda de Silva of Sri Lanka, Man of the Match.

Past Winners

1975 PRUDENTIAL CUP FINAL: Lord's, 21 June
West Indies 291-8 (60 overs. *Lloyd* 102, *Kanhai* 55, *Gilmour* 5 for 48). Australia 274 (58.4 overs. *I. M. Chappell* 62, *Boyce* 4 for 50).
West Indies won by 17 runs

1979 PRUDENTIAL CUP FINAL: Lord's, 23 June
West Indies 286-9 (60 overs. *Richards* 138no, *King* 86). England 194 (51 overs. *Brearley* 64, *Boycott* 57, *Garner* 5 for 38).
West Indies won by 92 runs

1983 PRUDENTIAL CUP FINAL: Lord's, 25 June
India 183 (54.5 overs). West Indies 140 (52 overs).
India won by 43 runs

1987 RELIANCE WORLD CUP FINAL: Eden Gardens, Calcutta, 8 November
Australia 253-5 (50 overs. *Boon* 75). England 246-8 (50 overs. *Athey* 58).
Australia won by 7 runs

1992 WORLD CUP FINAL: Melbourne Cricket Ground, 25 March
Pakistan 249-6 (50 overs. *Imran Khan* 72, *Javed Miandad* 58). England 227 (49.2 overs. *Fairbrother* 62).
Pakistan won by 22 runs

ICC Cricket World Cup trophy.

1996 WILLS WORLD CUP FINAL: Gaddafi Stadium, Lahore. 17 March

Sri Lanka won the toss

AUSTRALIA

M. A. Taylor c Jayasirya b de Silva	74
M. E. Waugh c Jayasirya b Vaas	12
R. T. Ponting b de Silva	45
S. R. Waugh c de Silva b Dharmasena	13
S. K. Warne st Kaluwitharana b Muralitharan	2
S. G. Law c de Silva b Jayasirya	22
M. G. Bevan not out	36
I. A. Healey b de Silva	2
P. R. Reiffel not out	13
D. W. Fleming	
G. D. McGrath	
Extras (lb10, w11, nb1)	22

Total (7 wickets; 50 overs) 241

Fall: 1-36, 2-137, 3-152, 4-156, 5-170, 6-202, 7-205
Bowling: Wickremsinghe 7-0-38-0, Vaas 6-1-30-1, Muralitharan 10-0-31-1, Dharmasena 10-0-47-1, Jayasirya 8-0-43-1, de Silva 9-0-42-3

SRI LANKA

S. T. Jayasirya run out	9
R. S. Kaluwitharana c Bevan b Fleming	6
A. R. Gurusinha b Reiffel	65
P. A. de Silva not out	107
A. Ranatunga not out	47
R. S. Mahanama	
H. P. Tillekeratne	
H. D. P. K. Dharmasena	
W. P. U. J. C. Vaas	
G. P. Wickremasinghe	
M. Muralitharan	
Extras (b1, lb4, w5, nb1)	11

Total (3 wickets; 46.2 overs) 245

Fall: 1-12, 2-23, 3-148

Bowling: McGrath 8.2-1-28-0, Fleming 6-0-43-1, Warne 10-0-58-0, Reiffel 10-0-49-1, M. E. Waugh 6-0-35-0, S. R. Waugh 3-0-15-0, Bevan 3-0-12-0

Umpires: S. A. Bucknor, D. R. Shepherd.
Match referee: C. H. Lloyd
Man of the match: P. A. de Silva

Sri Lanka won by 7 wickets.

GREAT PLAYERS
The Best 11 Players Ever

SIR JACK HOBBS, ENGLAND

Tests: 61

THE RIGHT OF Sir Jack
to be one of the first names
marked down in any all-
time World XI is not in
doubt. His first-class career
is, literally, without parallel.
Scorer of the most centuries
(197) and the most runs
(61,237) in the third-
highest number of innings
(1,315), with one of the
more competitive career
averages (50.65), Sir Jack
was the backbone of the
Surrey and England batting
line-ups for almost 30 years
until his retirement in 1934.
His 61-match Test career,
which ended in 1930 at the
age of 47 years eight

months, was equally impressive with 5,410 runs scored,
many of them made in partnership with Yorkshire's Herbert
Sutcliffe, at an average of 56.94. Nine of his 15 Test
centuries were made in Australia.

SUNIL GAVASKAR, INDIA
Tests: 125

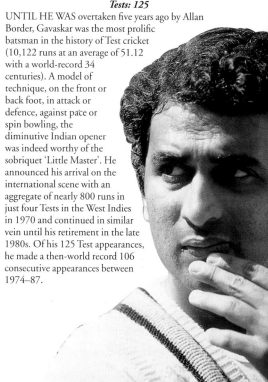

UNTIL HE WAS overtaken five years ago by Allan Border, Gavaskar was the most prolific batsman in the history of Test cricket (10,122 runs at an average of 51.12 with a world-record 34 centuries). A model of technique, on the front or back foot, in attack or defence, against pace or spin bowling, the diminutive Indian opener was indeed worthy of the sobriquet 'Little Master'. He announced his arrival on the international scene with an aggregate of nearly 800 runs in just four Tests in the West Indies in 1970 and continued in similar vein until his retirement in the late 1980s. Of his 125 Test appearances, he made a then-world record 106 consecutive appearances between 1974–87.

SIR DONALD BRADMAN, AUSTRALIA
Tests: 52

SIR DONALD BRADMAN is far and away the best batsman the game has ever seen. 'The Don' only failed to average more than 100 at the end of his Test career because he was bowled for a duck by England's Eric Hollies in his final innings for Australia at The Oval in 1948. His average of 99.94 and tally

of 6,996 runs (29 centuries) during a Test career which spanned 1928–48 was nevertheless a remarkable achievement. His overall first-class record is no less impressive – 28,067 runs at 95.14 with 117 centuries and a top-score of 452 not out (still the third highest individual innings of all time). With a record of 15 wins from 24 Tests in charge, he would also be a logical choice to captain our 'best ever' side.

DR W. G. GRACE, ENGLAND

Tests: 22

CRICKET'S FIRST 'SUPERSTAR', the Doctor was the main reason why the game became so popular during the 25 years before the First World War. Grace was in his thirties when he marked his England debut at The Oval in 1880 with a rousing 152 off Australia – against whom he played all his Tests. He tallied 126 first-class centuries, but made only one more for England. Even though his final Test in 1899 was just a month short of his 51st birthday and he was nearly 60 when he retired from first-class cricket, statistics only hint at his remarkable talents. He hit 54,896 runs (126 centuries), took 2,876 wickets and 887 catches, and regularly threw a ball more than 100 yards.

GRAEME POLLOCK, SOUTH AFRICA
Tests: 23

NO ALL-TIME XI would be complete without a high-quality left-hander near the top of the order. The numerous candidates for this position include the great Australians Harvey, Border and Morris, but had it not been for South Africa's political isolation throughout most of his career there seems little doubt that Graeme Pollock's career would have eclipsed them all. As it is, he managed an aggregate of 20,940 runs at 54.67 with 64

centuries despite being confined for most of his 26-year first-class career to the Currie Cup. But his brief Test career was also a dazzling one – 2,256 runs at 60.97 with seven hundreds, the highest of which was a truly marvellous 274 against Australia in Durban in the 1969–70 series.

SIR GARFIELD SOBERS, WEST INDIES
Tests: 93

SIR GARY IS generally regarded as cricket's greatest all-rounder. His international career, which spanned nearly 20 years, began when he was just 17 in 1953–54 against England. He went on to become the first batsman to top 8,000 Test runs, averaging 57.78 and counting a then-record 365 not out amongst his 26 centuries. His bowling, a mixture of pace, swing and slow left-arm, earned 235 wickets while his close-to-the-wicket fielding yielded 109 catches. But his captaincy, always adventurous, never quite matched up to his playing performances. One immortal piece of TV footage shows Sobers hitting Glamorgan's Malcolm Nash for six sixes off one over while playing for Nottinghamshire at Swansea in 1968.

IAN BOTHAM, ENGLAND
Tests: 102

FROM THE MOMENT Botham entered Test cricket with a five-wicket haul in an innings against Australia, he seemed destined for top billing. When he pulled the curtain down on his international career, not only did he leave some remarkable memories behind him but also an impressive array of statistics. His 383 Test wickets were complemented by 5,200 runs and 120 catches, nearly all taken at second slip. Only Sir Gary Sobers could claim to have a more impressive record as a Test all-rounder, but even the great West Indian would have been hard-pressed to trump Botham's finest hour at Leeds in 1981 when his unbeaten 149 helped England snatch victory from the jaws of defeat against Australia.

ALAN KNOTT, ENGLAND

Tests: 95

PICKING A WICKET-KEEPER for the all-time World XI was one of the toughest and most contentious of all our selections. The candidates included the Australian Rodney Marsh, the Jamaican Jeffrey Dujon, Pakistan's Wasim Bari and Godfrey Evans of England and Kent. But it is another man of Kent, the quicksilver Alan Knott, equally at home keeping to pace or spin, who gets the nod. Had he not been banned because of his involvement with Kerry Packer's World Series Cricket project in the late 1970s, Knott would have comfortably exceeded 100 Tests. He was also a valuable middle-order batsman whose counter-attacking approach rescued England from many a crisis.

MALCOLM MARSHALL, WEST INDIES
Tests: 81

EVEN THOUGH THIS side could give the new ball to either Sobers or Botham to swing and seam, there is still room for two specialist fast bowlers. The list of potential candidates, which includes Lindwall, Miller, Davidson, Trueman, Statham, Holding, Garner, Procter, Kahn, Hadlee and Kapil Dev, is enough to demonstrate the quality of the two 'quicks'

selected. Marshall, who took 376 Test wickets, comes out on top because, more than any other great fast bowler, he was impossible to subdue even in the most benign conditions. He was as fast as any bowler in the game, both through the air and (especially) off the pitch, economical to the point of meanness, able to cut the ball both ways and a master of late swing.

DENNIS LILLEE, AUSTRALIA
Tests: 70

IF CONTROLLED FEROCITY was Marshall's hallmark then Lillee's was classical simplicity. Rarely has a bowler looked as technically complete as Lillee at the point of delivery with a high, side-on action which enabled him to move the ball late both ways, off the pitch and in the air. Allied to his athleticism and strength was considerable courage, which was especially evident

as he battled back from a serious, career-threatening back injury to claim his place alongside Jeff Thomson and Max Walker in the Australian pace attack which destroyed all comers during the mid-1970s. His Test haul of 355 wickets meant that he averaged more than five wickets a match – a higher return than any of his rivals for a place in this team.

JIM LAKER, ENGLAND

Tests: 46

JIM LAKER WILL forever be remembered as the off-spinner who bowled Australia to a morale-crushing defeat at Old Trafford during the 1956 Ashes series with Test-record match figures of 19 for 90. Rarely can a bowler have dominated the opposition as Laker did that summer with a tally of 46 wickets at an average of just 9.60, although recent displays against Shane Warne and Muttiah Muralitharan show that English batsmen are just as vulnerable to high-class spin bowling. The Yorkshire-born Surrey bowler took a total of 193 wickets during a stop-start Test career which spanned 11 seasons but was often interrupted by selectorial quirks. In a first-class career from 1946–64, Laker took 1,944 wickets.

Those who came close to making the side:

Australia	Allan Border, Greg Chappell, Alan Davidson, Clarrie Grimmett, Ray Lindwall, Rodney Marsh, Keith Miller
England	Syd Barnes, Walter Hammond, Wilfred Rhodes, Brian Statham, Fred Trueman, Derek Underwood
West Indies	Joel Garner, Lance Gibbs, George Headley, Michael Holding, Viv Richards, Everton Weekes
South Africa	Barry Richards, Mike Procter
	Bishen Bedi,
India	Kapil Dev
Pakistan	Imran Khan
New Zealand	Richard Hadlee

The Best 11 Players Today

MIKE ATHERTON, ENGLAND

Tests: 84

FOLLOWING HIS ENGLAND debut against Australia at the age of 21, it was clear that this dogged Lancashire opener was on the fast track to greatness. His record 52-Test tenure as

England captain, from 1993–98, was a statistical failure although during the same period he confirmed his reputation as one of the most obdurate batsmen in Test cricket. After relinquishing the England captaincy to Alec Stewart, his batting form instantly returned with a haul of almost 500 runs in the home series against South Africa. Despite the classic opener's emphasis on defence, few batsmen possess a more cultured off-drive, either from the front or back foot.

ALEC STEWART, ENGLAND
Tests: 81

ONE OF CRICKET'S most naturally gifted strokeplayers, Stewart's early development as a Test player was, if anything, hampered by the fact that his father, Micky, was the England coach. Accusations of nepotism soon evaporated as it became clear what a skilful player Alec was. Currently the England captain, Stewart's Test career has been somewhat complicated by the fact that he is also a wicket-keeper of outstanding talent, albeit a part-time one. This Surrey stalwart's dual duties have meant a variety of positions in the batting order, from 1 to 7, but his present role as England's only genuine all-rounder earns him a place in this World XI.

SACHIN TENDULKAR, INDIA
Tests: 61

FROM THE MOMENT he made his Test debut in 1989 at the age of 16, it was clear that this stocky, wristy, little batsman had both the technique and temperament to become one of the game's top players well into the next millennium. Sir Donald Bradman, no less, has identified Tendulkar as the

modern batsman whom he believes is most similar to himself. Over the last year or so, since relinquishing the Indian captaincy, Tendulkar's figures have begun to assume Bradmanesque proportions. He is also the only Test batsman to have established a psychological advantage over Australia's master leg-spinner Shane Warne.

BRIAN LARA, WEST INDIES

Tests: 54

WHEN LARA SCORED a Test record 375 against England in Antigua in April 1994 and followed that up a few weeks later with 501 not out, a world record score for a first-class innings, for Warwickshire against Durham at Edgbaston, it seemed that the Trinidadian left-hander was destined to become the game's best batsman since Bradman. It was even felt Lara might eventually eclipse 'the Don', so prolific was his appetite for runs. But even though his eye is as sharp as ever and his backlift remains amazingly high, he lost form and has only recently shown signs of returning to his former majesty since taking over as West Indies captain.

ARAVINDA DE SILVA, SRI LANKA

Tests: 74

DESPITE DEBUTING AGAINST Pakistan while only a teenager, de Silva has been a late developer at Test level, partly because Sri Lanka played few international matches during his early years in the side. His 267 against New Zealand in 1991 finally marked him out as a mighty talent, but only recently has

he ground out runs consistently at the highest level to become his country's leading batsman with 17 Test centuries. He produced a match-winning century for Sri Lanka in the 1996 World Cup Final and capped a highly successful season for Kent the previous summer with a glorious hundred in a losing cause at Lord's in the Benson and Hedges Cup Final.

STEVE WAUGH, AUSTRALIA
Tests: 103

STEVE WAUGH HAS developed from being a promising
nippy change bowler who could bat a bit when he made his
Test debut in a modest Australian team at the age of 20 into
one of the hardest and most prolific middle-order batsmen in
world cricket, the backbone of probably the finest
international side currently playing the game. Waugh, whose
Test average is now around 50, owes his development to sheer
hard work and courage. Typically, his finest moment was
probably the 200 with which he tamed a hostile West Indies
pace attack at Sabina Park in 1995 and set up a rare Test series
victory for Australia in the Caribbean.

CARL HOOPER, WEST INDIES

Tests: 73

FOR MUCH OF HIS career, this gifted West Indian all-rounder has been something of an enigma, often under-achieving with the bat after an initial blaze of brilliant strokes or throwing his wicket away when required to apply himself. But after five prolific seasons with Kent, during which his wily, skilfully floated off-spin bowling has become an increasingly important part of the county's attack, his batting appears to have matured and the West Indies are now reaping the benefit in the form of heavier and more consistent scoring. Without question, Hooper is one of the game's most exciting players, a guaranteed box-office attraction.

WASIM AKRAM, PAKISTAN

Tests: 79

DESPITE THE dents inflicted on his reputation by ongoing feuds in Pakistani cricket, Wasim Akram, who made his debut at 18, is undeniably the most successful left-arm bowler in Test history, his total approaching 350 wickets. His fast-bowling armoury includes a fearsome bouncer and devastating yorker (the ability to swing and seam the ball both ways) and a beautifully disguised slower delivery. He is equally destructive with the bat as an unbeaten 257 against Zimbabwe in 1996 demonstrated. But the responsibilities of leading the attack plus captaining both Pakistan and Lancashire mean that he rarely fulfils his batting potential.

SHANE WARNE, AUSTRALIA

Tests: 67

WARNE IS PERHAPS the most exciting and masterful bowler of modern times. Despite his unexpected mauling by India's batsmen in 1998 after five years of uninterrupted dominance, Warne still took enough wickets in that series to overtake Lance Gibbs and become the most prolific wicket-taking spinner in Test cricket. His marvellous array of deliveries – at least three different types of leg-spinner, a variety of googlys (balls which go on with the arm) and a wicked top-spinner – have mesmerised and bemused a succession of seasoned batsmen and been largely instrumental in establishing Australia as today's leading Test nation.

CURTLY AMBROSE, WEST INDIES
Tests: 80

ENGLAND FANS STILL wince at the memory of how, in March 1994, Mike Atherton's men needed only 194 runs to pull off a famous victory over the West Indies in Trinidad only to be blown away for 46 with Ambrose taking 6 for 24. The

6 ft 7 in Antiguan has led the West Indian attack since 1987 and his haul of 330 plus Test wickets has been achieved at an astonishingly economical rate. Ambrose is a fierce competitor, a miserly bowler when conditions do not suit him and simply devastating when they do. Even in the twilight of his career, he remains the benchmark for all aspiring fast bowlers.

ALLAN DONALD, SOUTH AFRICA
Tests: 47

WITH THE GRACE AND athleticism of a gazelle and the lethal ferocity of a cheetah, Allan Donald is the ultimate fast bowler. His pace matches that of anyone who has ever played the game, and his unquenchable competitiveness make him the ideal strike bowler for a captain, always willing to turn his

arm over in his side's quest for a vital wicket. He is the single biggest reason why South Africa has returned so effectively to the international fold following the demise of Apartheid. Donald's 'average' of five wickets per Test puts him on a par with two of the greatest fast bowlers of all time – Dennis Lillee and Richard Hadlee.

Note: A notional 16-strong squad to represent Earth on tour to Mars would probably also include:

Sanath Jayasuriya, Sri Lanka
Tests: 38
Left-hand opening bat, slow left-arm bowler

Shaun Pollock, South Africa
Tests: 25
Right-hand middle-order batsman, right-arm fast bowler

Ian Healy, Australia
Tests: 103
Wicket-keeper, right-hand middle-order batsman

Muttiah Muralitharan, Sri Lanka
Tests: 42
Right arm off-spinner

Waqar Younis, Pakistan
Tests: 53
Right-arm fast bowler

(Statistics accurate to the end of the 1998 English season.)

The 10 Most Memorable Moments

IAN BOTHAM'S 149 NOT OUT AGAINST AUSTRALIA AT HEADINGLEY, 1981

BOTHAM'S BRIEF SPELL as England captain ended after losing the first Test of the series at Trent Bridge and bagging a pair in the drawn second at Lord's. Mike Brearley returned to lead the side at Headingley, but for the first three-and-a-half days the game went Australia's way and an innings defeat for England looked certain. At 135 for 7, they were still 92 behind when Botham, who earlier took six wickets, was joined at the crease by Graham Dilley. The pair added 117, with Dilley hitting 56, then Botham put on a further 67 with Chris Old. When last man Bob Willis was dismissed on the final morning, Australia required 130 to win. But Willis took 8 for 43 as England claimed the unlikeliest of victories by 18 runs and went on to take the series 3–1.

Brian Lara with Sir Garfield Sobers after setting his new record.

BRIAN LARA'S 375 AGAINST ENGLAND, 1994

ENGLAND WENT INTO the Fifth Test against the West Indies at St John's, Antigua on 16 April 1994 in a fairly positive frame of mind. Although they had lost the series having been defeated in the first three Tests, they had won the Fourth Test by 208 runs. At St John's, the home side batted first and Brian Lara came in to bat at 10.32 on the first morning. The 24-year-old Trinidadian batsman started to work the bowlers to all corners of the park. On the third day at 11.46 am, Lara pulled a ball to the boundary to pass the 365 mark – Sir Garfield Sobers' long-standing individual Test record. Sir Gary himself came on to the field to congratulate Lara, who went on to make 375 off 536 balls.

BRIAN LARA'S 501 NOT OUT AGAINST DURHAM AT EDGBASTON, 1994

SHORTLY AFTER SCORING his magnificent 375 against England, Brian Lara was back playing for Warwickshire in the County Championship and his rich vein of form continued, culminating on 6 June 1994 when he became the first batsman in first-class cricket to reach 500 in a single innings. As Lara began to accumulate his runs against a hapless Durham attack

at Edgbaston, word began to spread that history was in the making at the Birmingham ground, and the crowd grew steadily. Lara never looked like getting out and time appeared to be the only obstacle to the young batting star again rewriting the record books. He reached his target when he smashed a ball to the off-side boundary and finished on 501 not out off just 427 balls.

Brian Lara celebrates his 501 not out, 1994.

JIM LAKER'S 19 FOR 90 AGAINST AUSTRALIA AT OLD TRAFFORD, 1956

ENGLAND'S DEFENCE of the Ashes had been far from uneventful when, with the series poised at one Test apiece and one drawn, the old adversaries pitched up to Old Trafford for the fourth encounter of a five-match series. No bowler had ever taken 18 wickets in a first-class match before, but Jim Laker, the Yorkshire-born Surrey off-spinner, was to indelibly rewrite the record books. After England had accumulated 459, Laker blew the Australians away for 84, capturing every wicket except for Jim Burke, who fell to his county colleague Tony Lock.

Inclement weather ensured that Australia's second innings extended through to Tuesday afternoon when Colin McDonald provided the prodigious spinner with his 19th wicket of the match as England clinched victory by an innings and 170 runs.

Jim Laker, who captured 19 Australian wickets in 1956.

SIR GARY SOBERS HITTING SIX SIXES OFF ONE OVER AT SWANSEA, 1968

GARFIELD SOBERS was at the peak of his powers in 1968. He was the greatest West Indian Test player of all time and

probably the finest all-rounder in the game's history. He held a number of records, including the highest individual Test score of 365 not out – a total Brian Lara was to surpass in 1994. Playing for Nottinghamshire against Glamorgan at Swansea, Sobers took guard as left-arm spinner Malcolm Nash prepared to bowl a new over. Six balls and much excitement later, another record belonged to Sobers – six sixes off one six-ball over. India's Ravi Shastri repeated the feat in 1985 when he hit 36 off an over from Tilak Raj when playing for Bombay against Baroda.

FRED TRUEMAN'S 300TH TEST WICKET
AT THE OVAL, 1964

HAVING BEEN DROPPED along with Colin Cowdrey for
Old Trafford, Trueman was recalled at the age of 33 for the
final Test at The Oval. England, 1–0 down at the time, were
bowled out for 182 and the Australians reached 343 for 6 on
the third morning. Trueman then dismissed Ian Redpath and
Graham McKenzie with successive deliveries immediately
before lunch. He failed to complete his hat-trick after the
interval, but later had Neil Hawke caught by Cowdrey at slip
to become the first bowler to take 300 Test wickets. He
wrapped up the Australian innings for 379 when Graham
Corling became his 301st victim. In England's second innings
of 381 for 4 (the final day was washed out), Cowdrey
completed 5,000 Test runs.

Fred Trueman, centre, takes his 300th Test wicket, 1964.

DEREK UNDERWOOD BOWLING
ENGLAND TO VICTORY AGAINST
AUSTRALIA AT THE OVAL, 1968

ENGLAND'S EFFORTS to regain the Ashes were thwarted in 1968 by the weather. After losing at Old Trafford, rain undermined them at Lord's and Edgbaston. In the final Test at The Oval, it again looked as though the climate would have the final say. Thanks to centuries by John Edrich and Basil d'Oliveira, England set Australia 352 to win and at lunch on the last day, Kent's left-arm spinner Derek Underwood had reduced them to 85 for 5. The pitch was then flooded by a storm and when the sun came out an army of spectators helped the ground staff mop up so that the final 75 minutes could be played. After stout Australian resistance, Underwood took the last four wickets to seal England's victory with six minutes left.

Derek Underwood takes England to victory, 1968.

ENGLAND WINNING BACK THE ASHES
AT THE OVAL, 1953

AFTER FOUR DRAWS of varying quality during a wet summer, England regained the Ashes, held by Australia for the past 20 years, in the final Test at The Oval. The ground was packed with a capacity 30,000 crowd each day and hopes rose when England dismissed Australia for 275 – a total that would have been much lower had Ray Lindwall not thrashed 62 late-order runs. A rearguard action inspired by Trevor Bailey gave England a first-innings lead of 31 before the Surrey spin – twins Jim Laker and Tony Lock bowled out Australia for 162 second time round. England, set 132 to win, clinched victory on the fourth afternoon when Denis Compton scored the winning run and dispelled the gloom that had hung over English cricket since the end of the Second World War.

The England team before winning back the Ashes, 1953.

SHANE WARNE BOWLING
MIKE GATTING WITH 'THAT BALL', 1993

THE AUSTRALIAN TOURING party of 1993 relied heavily on leg-spinner Shane Warne and there was much media speculation as to how the England batsmen would cope with his bowling. The First Test was at Old Trafford and Mike Gatting, who had been a good player of spin throughout his career, was at the receiving end when Warne came on to bowl. The was near-silence around the ground and the television pundits were examining the bowler's movements in minute

detail. Gatting took guard and Warne started his short, but determined, run-up to the wicket. The ball pitched on or just outside leg stump, Gatting played a routine forward defensive push but the ball spun viciously and lifted, beat the bat and hit the top of the off stump. Gatting and those watching could not believe their eyes. They had witnessed one of the great balls bowled in Test cricket.

PETER MAY AND COLIN COWDREY'S MATCH-SAVING STAND AGAINST THE WEST INDIES, 1957

THE FIRST TEST AT Edgbaston saw England bowled out for 186 with the spinner Sonny Ramadhin taking 7 for 49. The visitors then piled on 474 thanks to a majestic 161 from Collie Smith (who was tragically killed in a car accident two years later). When Colin Cowdrey joined his captain Peter May early on the fourth morning with three wickets down, England's plight looked hopeless. But it was a further eight hours and 20 minutes before the West Indies struck again as May and Cowdrey shared a historic partnership of 411. When Cowdrey went for 154, England were safe and May declared shortly afterwards, unbeaten on 285. Not only did England finish on top but Ramadhin took only five more wickets as his side lost the series.

Peter May.

Best Batsmen and Bowlers Since 1976–77

VIV RICHARDS, WEST INDIES
Tests: 121

RICHARDS EMERGED FROM Antigua in the Leeward Islands to become the most destructive batsman of his era and to captain the West Indies in 50 Tests. His tally of 8,540 Test runs, at an average of 50.23, included 24 centuries, the highest

of which was the 291 he plundered off a respectable England attack at The Oval in 1976, his *annus mirabilis*. Richards, who was built like a light-heavyweight boxer and batted with the power of one, also starred for most of the 1970s and 1980s with

Somerset before ending his county career with Glamorgan. To his tally of 114 first-class centuries, the most ever compiled by a Caribbean batsman, should be added several ferocious one-day performances, including an astonishing unbeaten 189 against England at Old Trafford in 1984, which stood as the highest international limited-overs innings for nearly 13 years. His flat off-spin bowling was useful in one-day cricket, while his sharp reflexes rewarded him with 122 Test catches, mainly in the slips.

IMRAN KHAN, PAKISTAN

Tests: 88

IN ANY OTHER ERA this superb cricketer, who captained Pakistan in 48 Tests, would have been hailed as the greatest all-rounder of his generation. But, almost as a freak of nature, the game threw up not one but four magnificent all-rounders who were at the peak of their powers at the same time. The other three were Ian Botham, Richard Hadlee and Kapil Dev, all fast or seam bowlers and spectacular middle-order batsmen, and in truth Imran's record compares favourably with theirs. His bowling, which had progressed from accurate military medium in the early 1970s to genuine hostility when he returned to Test cricket after his spell with Kerry Packer, earned him 362 Test wickets at an average of 22.81 – more than five and a half runs cheaper than Botham. His batting produced 3,807 Test runs at an average of 37.69 – again better than Botham – though his haul of six Test centuries would undoubtedly have been higher had he not played in such a strong batting line-up.

SIR RICHARD HADLEE, NEW ZEALAND

Tests: 86

SHEER HARD WORK, dedication and a detailed study of the techniques of fast bowling triggered a remarkable

transformation in Sir Richard during his mid-20s. When the young New Zealander took his first faltering steps on the international stage, he was a raw, somewhat over-enthusiastic bowler with a tendency to either overpitch or give the batsman

prior warning when about to attempt a bouncer. But towards the end of the 1970s, helped to a great extent by his years with Nottinghamshire, he suddenly developed into a classical fast bowler with an economical run-up and a naggingly accurate off-stump line. The results were astonishing as Hadlee struck terror into the hearts of the most accomplished batsmen, unsure which way the ball would seam off the pitch, and piled up 431 Test scalps. He carried the New Zealand attack for more than a decade while his pugnacious left-handed batting, which produced 3,124 Test runs, also gave the Kiwis genuine middle-order backbone.

Explanation of Rankings

The question of who the best players in the world are has been asked since Test cricket began and arguments have no doubt raged as a consequence of a cricket enthusiast trying to explain his chosen list of top players to another 'amateur' selector.

CRICKET IS A GAME of statistics and endless comparisons of batting and bowling averages are one way of selecting the top players.

But averages can be misleading. Graeme Hick has a good Test record overall for England, but has struggled to make runs regularly on the international stage against top-class fast bowling. He plunders runs from some teams but has failed against others.

To help assess the current form of players, the Deloitte Ratings were introduced in 1987. These ranked cricketers on a scale up to 1,000 according to their performances in Test matches. Variables such as the result of the match, playing conditions and the quality of the opposition are taken into account. Once all the data is loaded onto the computer, a specially written software package does the rest. The rankings are then sent out to the media and the debate as to who is the best is fuelled once again.

Golf has its own system of rating competitors – the Sony World Rankings – and there is always interest shown by tennis fans as to who is the current world number one in their sport. The systems used to produce golf and tennis rankings also take factors other than merely results into account.

Now known as the PricewaterhouseCoopers Ratings, assessments of Test and one-day-international teams (on a scale of up to 100) are also produced.

1998 RANKINGS

The latest rankings based on matches played up to 30 November 1998 are as follows:

Batsmen

Rating

1 *S. R. Waugh* (Australia) 836
2 *S. R. Tendulkar* (India) 822
3 *R. S. Dravid* (India) 796
4 *B. C. Lara* (West Indies) 767
5 *S. Anwar* (Pakistan) 762
6 *W. J. Cronje* (South Africa) 741
7 *M. E. Waugh* (Australia) 735
8 *P. A. de Silva* (Sri Lanka) 734
9 *S. Chanderpaul* (West Indies) 720
10 *A. J. Stewart* (England) 706

Bowlers

Rating

1 *A. A. Donald* (South Africa) 873
2 *C. E. L. Ambrose* (West Indies) 864
3 *S. M. Pollock* (South Africa) 824
4 *G. D. McGrath* (Australia) 810
5 *M. Muralitharan* (Sri Lanka) 787
6 *A. R. C. Fraser* (England) 755
7 *A. Kumble* (India) 749
8 *Wasim Akram* (Pakistan) 728
9 *S. K. Warne* (Australia) 720
10 *Waqar Younis* (Pakistan) 712

The latest rankings based on matches played up to 31 August 1998 are as follows:

International ratings
Test matches

1	Australia	64
2	Pakistan	61
3	South Africa	57
4	India	53
5	West Indies	47
6	Sri Lanka	47
7	England	37
8	New Zealand	29
9	Zimbabwe	15

One-day internationals
Rating

1	South Africa	65
2	Sri Lanka	63
3	West Indies	59
4	Australia	57
5	India	53
6	England	50
7	Pakistan	45
8	New Zealand	39
9	Zimbabwe	25

PLAYING THE GAME
How and Where to Start

One of the problems facing anyone wishing to play cricket in Britain is the unpredictable weather. Unlike most other countries that play top-class cricket, our climate does not encourage youngsters to practice outdoors hour after hour, day after day as the legendary Australian Sir Donald Bradman did when he was learning the skills of the game.

IN THE CARIBBEAN, practising on the beaches or in the fields seems much more attractive than playing outdoors on a cold and wet English summer's day. India, Pakistan and Sri Lanka also have dry, warm climates to encourage young players to practice their skills outdoors.

Junior cricket in Antigua.

Under 11 village cricket, England.

POPULARITY OF CRICKET

DESPITE THE WEATHER, cricket remains a popular sport in Britain and in recent years the financial rewards for top-class professional players have improved significantly. Cricketers still earn much less than footballers and many other top sportsmen but their salaries have increased thanks to sponsorship and income from broadcasting.

In Britain, schools and local clubs traditionally offer the opportunity for youngsters to take up and participate in organised cricket. But cricket played at schoolboy level can be totally different to that experienced at local club level where the matches can be far more competitive and young players can find themselves up against bigger and stronger adults. However, this environment can also provide a 'fast-track' development for the young cricketer who has the basic skills and desire to go on and play at a higher level.

When and Where to Play

For those who want to play cricket as a more recreational sport, turning out for a club's Second or Third Eleven can be just as rewarding – the social side of cricket cannot be over-estimated.

Kwik Cricket.

IN ADDITION to school and cricket club facilities, local sports centres can often provide indoor nets and help with coaching. There is also the opportunity to play indoor cricket throughout the winter months and improve or maintain your general level of health and fitness.

CRICKET IN SCHOOLS

THERE HAS been much criticism of some local education authorities in recent years over the lack of money and provision for cricket in schools. The policy of selling off school playing fields has left many schools with few or no cricketing facilities of their own.

Cricket is played for just one term in schools and unfortunately it coincides with summer examinations. School pupils, and indeed teachers, often have difficulty in finding enough time to dedicate to the game.

Despite all the problems, playing in school matches is an ideal early opportunity for young cricketers to develop their talents. Good players can be noticed and selected to play for their county schools sides. The outstanding young cricketer can even go on and play for the England schools teams.

First-class county clubs usually have initiatives with local schools that involve special coaching and practice sessions. Obviously, the counties see contact with schools as a way of identifying possible county players of the future.

School cricket, London.

Cricket Clubs

If a school has few or no cricketing facilities a young person would not have the experience of playing cricket as part of a team in an organised match. The option, therefore, is to join a local club that best suits your requirements.

Village cricket is regarded by many as the lifeblood of the sport.

SMALL TOWNS and villages usually have at least one club and the choice, although limited, is probably an easier one to make in more rural areas than in the bigger cities and conurbations.

Cricket clubs often advertise for new members on public library noticeboards or in local newspapers. Lists of clubs are also usually available in libraries.

The National Cricket Association (NCA) was set up in 1965 with the objective of aiding and encouraging all cricket that was not accorded first-class status. Since 1 January 1997, the England and Wales Cricket Board (ECB) has been responsible for the administration of all cricket – professional and recreational – and as a consequence has taken on the function of the NCA.

Advice on local clubs in your area and details of the ECB's various initiatives involving the county clubs can be obtained

by contacting them at the address given at the end of this book.

The authorities have also recently introduced the game of *Kwik Cricket* – a form of cricket played with a larger, soft ball and designed to encourage young girls and boys to take an interest in the sport. Details of *Kwik Cricket* can also be obtained from the ECB.

Kwik Cricket, Old Trafford.

PLAYING CLUB CRICKET

Once you have selected and joined your club you may find the atmosphere of a cricket game totally different from school matches or the improvised games played with your friends.

BECAUSE YOU WILL be playing with more experienced and probably better players than yourself you may not bat as high up in the order or bowl as many overs as you are used to – the young cricketer has to learn patience.

You may have been a solid all-rounder for your school but your club coach or captain may see you as having more potential as an opening or middle-order batsman. Conversely, you may be advised to concentrate on your bowling, maybe even changing from a seam bowler to an off-spinner. Also, once you have joined a club you may be asked to help out at the ground with some of the basic chores such as putting up and taking down the nets, sweeping the pavilion or setting out the boundary pegs. But this is all part of being a member of a local cricket club. You may even be asked to help out on the administration side – the roles of a club secretary or fixtures secretary can be thankless!

However, once you are a *bona fide* member of a club the rewards can be limitless not only in cricketing terms but also from a social point of view.

Essex celebrating winning the Benson and Hedges Cup, 1998.

Kit Requirements

One of the reasons why young people may hesitate before taking up cricket seriously, or indeed make an older person think twice about returning to the sport, is the idea that the basic kit required is expensive. If every item of kit purchased was top of the range, that could be the case. However, a young cricketer need not buy the most expensive items on the market.

The basic clothing and equipment required is:

- **shirt**
- **trousers**
- **sweater**
- **bat**
- **pads**
- **batting gloves**
- **footwear**
- **protector (or 'box')**
- **thigh pad**
- **cap or sun hat**
- **helmet**

The most basic equipment.

CLOTHING

SHIRTS, TROUSERS, sweaters and footwear retail at varied prices. But for the weekend cricketer, unlike his first-class counterpart, these are not tools of the trade, and it is not always necessary, or sensible, to buy the most expensive items on the market.

Magazines such as *The Cricketer* will carry a number of

advertisements offering discounted cricket clothing and equipment. Also, it is likely the local club will have some sort of arrangement with a retail outlet that makes good quality cricket clothing available at discount prices.

Choice of footwear, as with most items of kit, is usually based on personal preference and comfort. Most shoes are made of leather with spiked soles, but some players prefer to wear full dimpled rubber-sole shoes – especially in dry conditions. When buying a new pair of cricket shoes remember to select a pair under which you can wear thick socks.

Andy Flower of Zimbabwe, fully kitted-out.

EQUIPMENT

MOST CLUBS WILL provide a cricket bag containing the basic equipment required by a young cricketer – including bats, pads and gloves. Although it is not always desirable to use a pair of batting gloves straight after somebody else has used them, the provision of the cricket bag does mean the young cricketer does not have to purchase all his clothing and equipment at the start of his time with his club.

BATS

THE BAT IS LIKELY to be the single most expensive piece of equipment bought by a young person – and the most crucial.

There are two types of bat – natural and polyarmoured. The trend nowadays is for heavier bats, but these do not always suit a young player. When assessing a new bat's suitability, it is important to judge the pick-up weight. Pick it up with the top hand only to see if you can manage a high and correct backlift.

Find a bat that suits you.

Most bats are made with short handles, but some taller players prefer the rarer long-handled bat. Make certain the grip is firm and the rubber tube casing on the handle is in good condition.

A new natural bat (made of willow) should be given a light treatment of linseed oil once a week for the first four months and then once a month thereafter.

Before using a new bat in a match it should be 'knocked-in' by bouncing a leather cricket ball on the hitting area to help harden the surface.

A polyarmoured bat is ready to use when you buy it and does not need oiling. To take care of this type of bat all you need do is wipe the blade with a clean cloth after use.

Ready to bat.

BALLS

THE QUALITY OF cricket balls used in club cricket can vary enormously. Top quality balls have a cork cube in the middle, and alternate layers of cork and wool are wound around it until a sphere of the correct shape and size is achieved. This is then covered in leather and a continuous seam is stitched around the outside. A ball good enough to be used at first-class level is expensive and in club cricket cheaper two- or even one-piece balls are sometimes used. You may even find yourself using a ball that has seen action in previous matches.

Balls used at senior level weigh 5 ½–5 ¾ oz (155–163 g) and have a circumference of between 8 ¹³⁄₁₆–9 in (22.4–22.9 cm). Smaller balls are allowed to be used in junior matches and women's cricket.

In most matches a red ball is used but in day/night matches played under floodlights, a white ball has been introduced.

PROTECTIVE EQUIPMENT

WHATEVER THE quality and age of a cricket ball it is still likely to be hard enough to hurt you if it hits you and that is why selecting the correct protective equipment is so important.

Protective equipment is essential.

PADS

PADS ARE ESSENTIAL items of kit: they protect the legs from the ball if it beats the bat. They are usually made of either canvas or buckskin outers over cane and sidewing padding. Most pads will also have two or three additional foam-filled sections around the knee area for extra protection. When choosing pads, make sure you select the correct size and most comfortable design.

Pads must be worn.

GLOVES

BATTING GLOVES ARE also essential for a batsman, as they greatly reduce the risk of injuries to the hands, especially if you are facing fast bowling or batting on a pitch that suddenly sees

a delivery rear up nastily. There are many types of gloves made nowadays. The design favoured by cricketers at all levels has a leather pad on the palm to ensure a good grip of the bat and foam-filled

Gloves will prevent hand injuries.

protectors on the back of the glove. Inner gloves are sometimes worn to give additional protection.

ADDITIONAL EQUIPMENT

THE PROTECTOR or 'box' should always be worn to protect a batsman's most delicate area. Thigh and arm pads are worn increasingly and are made of canvas over a polystyrene padded protector.

The batsman's helmet is seen at an increasing number of matches, and although a necessary protection against fast bowlers on suspect pitches, this headgear is rather costly.

Fitness Tips

BACKGROUND

DIET AND FITNESS have been subjects high on the agenda for all walks of life in the past 20 years or so. The jogging boom of the 1970s and the proliferation of local health clubs have highlighted the impression – real or concocted by the marketing men – that the general public is genuinely interested in eating the right things and exercising in a correct and safe manner.

Cricket had for many years been seen, even at first-class level, as a game for technique rather than fitness. However, the sport has changed significantly and now power, strength and stamina are all prerequisites for a player at any level.

At senior level, one of the most notable developments has been the extraordinary improvement in the standard of fielding – or at least in the art of run saving. This has been caused in the main by the demands of one-day, limited-overs cricket, where literally every run counts. However, the demands on a cricketer's fitness, or at least his attitude to his own eating and drinking habits have in the past left a lot to be desired.

W. G. Grace was renowned for his fondness for food. Major James Gilman, a team-mate of the great man, recalling a match played at Crystal Palace against the first West Indian touring party, told how W. G. 'was very keen on the catering'. He added that the Doctor had: 'a sumptuous lunch, with hock and claret on the table. He had a real whack of the roast, followed by a big lump of cheese. He also tackled his whisky and seltzer, which was always his drink.'

The England team training, 1997.

CRICKETERS AND FITNESS

Maurice Tate, one of the best seam bowlers of all time, is said to have always drunk a couple pints of Guinness at lunchtime to 'recharge his batteries' for a long bowling spell in the afternoon.

MORE RECENTLY MUCH has been said and written about ex-England wicket-keeper Jack Russell's eccentric eating habits, especially the food he insists on taking overseas on tours. But he was a one-off and without doubt the days are long gone when teams had stodgy food as a rule for lunch. Nowadays you are more likely to find salads and perhaps pasta on the menu when players return to the pavilion for their lunch break: the professional cricketer appreciates the benefits of good, healthy

eating. A good diet is only part of the battle for full fitness, however. Players are paying more attention to their drinking habits as well.

Gone are the days when professional cricketers would turn up at the club for pre-season nets just a few days before the first match. Today, the modern professional cricketer keeps himself fit throughout the year. Graham Gooch, who has recently retired from the game was a good example of the first-class player's desire to keep fit. The former England captain was a big man, but kept to a strict fitness regime that included circuit training and jogging. He even trained with his local professional football club, West Ham United, in the winter months in his desire to keep fit.

England warm up before a match.

FITNESS TODAY

It is not unusual to turn up at a county match an hour or so before the scheduled start and see the teams exercising on the field. Years ago players just indulged themselves in a little fielding and catching practice but today, you are more likely to see them participating in a group stretching exercise as well as a host of running routines.

FORMER ENGLAND skipper and fast bowler Bob Willis, who stands more than 6 ft 6 in, had a most bizarre stretching programme. But it worked for him, and if performed properly can still save a bowler from potential injury.

A young player just taking up cricket will have the natural fitness of youth but must work on areas that can be strengthened by hard work and determination. Stamina can be built up with the aid of long distance running – a number of first-class counties have added distance running to their pre-season training sessions.

PREPARING FOR THE GAME

KEEPING THE muscles warm is also a vital part of ensuring on-going fitness. A gentle warm-up before a game is essential. It is also as important to 'warm down' as it is to 'warm up'. That is why bowlers will put on a sweater at the end of each over and why a batsman will shower and change his kit after a long innings.

Training in the swimming pool.

TRAINING SESSIONS

Physical fitness also aids mental discipline. The right attitude to the game is certainly developed if the player's body is fine-tuned. Mentally, a player can go down if he is tired, but it is easier to drive his game forward if he is fit and healthy.

IF YOU CANNOT make it to your school or club's fitness and training sessions, do your own exercises at home or, better still, go to your local gym. However, always seek advice on the fitness routines that would best suit your needs. It is just as dangerous for a young person to rush into a series of unscheduled and unsuitable exercises as it is for an older person doing physical activity for the first time in years.

The time and effort spent on achieving and maintaining a good level of fitness will always be worthwhile. A sensible approach to eating and drinking will also be rewarded. If you can develop the perfect mix of good technique and fitness, you will get more enjoyment from the game of cricket and no doubt achieve more success as a consequence.

A training run for the England team, New Zealand.

Becoming an Umpire

Harold 'Dickie' Bird has recently retired as a first-class umpire and over the years he has become the best-known 'man in the white coat' in the world.

ONE OF THE great emotional moments in cricket of recent times was the reception given to Bird as he walked from the pavilion at Lord's in June 1996 for his last appearance as a Test match umpire. The England–India Test was his 66th and this remains a world record for an umpire at that level.

Dickie Bird rules lbw.

Most people who are persuaded, or indeed volunteer, to stand as umpires remain quite anonymous and at school and club level, there is often little pressure put on the match officials. That is not the case now in Tests and one-day internationals where every decision is scrutinised in minute detail by constant televised action replays.

Top-class umpires are usually former players and Test match officials are often former internationals – although in Bird's case, he never played for England and had only a moderate first-class playing record.

Young people wishing to take up umpiring at an early age are advised to contact their local county association – which is usually based at the county side's main ground. Courses in umpiring are organised throughout Britain.

For more advice you can contact the Association of Cricket Umpires and Scorers (details given in Useful Addresses, p. 251).

A third umpire watching the monitor.

Techniques

BOWLING

THERE ARE FOUR basic requirements for young players to master if they are to become successful bowlers – fast or slow. These are:

- **Grip of the ball**
- **Run-up**
- **Delivery**
- **Follow-through**

A good grip will help you control the ball.

Grip of the ball

It is vital that a bowler has a sound grip of the ball as he delivers it. There are a variety of grips to suit different types of bowlers, but the most basic grip involves the first two fingers of the bowling hand being held alongside the seam, slightly apart. The inside of the thumb rests on the seam directly below the first two fingers on the opposite side of the ball. The third finger rests against the ball, simply as a support. This basic grip will give the bowler control of the ball, but remember to hold the ball with your fingers and not the palm of your hand.

Run-up

The run-up is probably the most neglected aspects of a bowler's technique and it is essential that a young player, whether a fast bowler or spinner, gets his run-up absolutely right.

Long run-ups are used by fast bowlers to give them speed and momentum at the point of delivery. Fluent, though shorter, run-ups are required by slow bowlers if they are to bowl consistently well.

Always pace out the number of strides you are going to take from the wicket to the start of your run-up. Make a mark at that point to ensure your run-up is the same for each delivery. If you find you are arriving at the wicket either too soon or too

late, change the position of the marker. Practice your run-up before you bowl your first delivery of a new spell.

Keep your head still during your run-up and focus on the intended part of the wicket where you want the ball to pitch. Concentrate on your rhythm: inexperienced bowlers make the mistake of running in too fast and they lose control.

A perfect run-up is the result of months of practice: Dennis Lillee.

Delivery

When you arrive at the wicket your left shoulder should be pointing at the batsman taking guard, with your left arm above your head.

At this stage your weight should be on your back foot, but as the ball is delivered the weight should be transferred to the leading left leg.

The bowling arm is swung forward and the left arm moves in the opposite direction. At the point of delivery, the back leg is raised off the ground to start the follow-through.

Curtley Ambrose demonstrates the perfect delivery.

An unusual bowling style from Paul Adams.

Follow-through

Natural momentum will cause a bowler to take a few more strides down the wicket after releasing the ball. In an effort not to damage the pitch with the follow-through, steps should be taken as far to the side of the wicket as possible. A bowler who continually runs down the centre of the pitch after delivering the ball is in danger of being banned by the umpires from bowling again in the innings.

Follow-through: Paul Adams, Saqlain Mushtaq and Shane Warne.

Types of Bowling

> Remember that the four basic requirements for good
> bowling apply to all bowling styles.

PACE BOWLING

MANY YOUNG cricketers dream of becoming fast bowlers
and emulate today's superstars such as South Africa's Allan
Donald, but only a few will have the physical requirements to
succeed. Fast bowlers generally rely on sheer pace to dismiss
batsmen either by bowling a full-length ball in an attempt to
clean bowl the batsman, have him caught behind the wicket or
given out lbw. The fast bowler can also bowl short and hope for
a catch close to the wicket off the bat or gloves.

The bouncer – a fast ball pitched halfway down the wicket
– is another option and the batsman, apart from being
'roughed-up' by such a delivery, could also be tempted to hook
the ball in the air and be caught in the deep. A fast bowler can
also try a heavily-disguised slower delivery and hope the
batsman plays too early and offers a catch. Most young bowlers

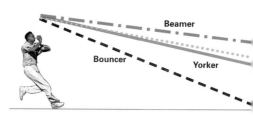

at school level try and bowl as fast as they can, and in most cases they fail simply because they lose control. The main rule for any emerging fast bowler should be to aim at the stumps. Learn to bowl straight from the start – you can always add extra pace as you develop.

Pace bowlers can make the ball bounce in different places down the pitch to test the batsman.

Beamer: considered dangerous and ungentlemanly; quite rare

Full toss: bad ball – doesn't quite bounce; quite easy to hit

Yorker: bounces up by batsman's feet, trying to go under his bat

Bouncer: bounces halfway down wicket; rears up to batsman's head

Half volley (not pictured): bounces a little closer to bowler than yorker; easy to hit

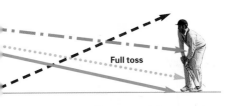

Full toss

INSWINGERS AND OUTSWINGERS

SOME BOWLERS have a natural ability to swing the ball in the air. The ball is delivered at a slower pace – the longer the ball is in the air the more time it has to swing. A delivery swings as a result of atmospheric conditions, the direction the seam is pointing and the amount of shine on the ball. Usually only one half of the ball is continually polished by the bowler and fielders, while the other half is left to lose its shine.

To bowl an inswinger – a ball that swings from the off-side to leg-side – the seam should be pointing to leg and the shiny part of the ball facing the off. The ball should be bowled on a

full length, on or just outside the off stump. The outswinger does the opposite and swings in the air to the off. The seam is aimed at first slip with the shiny part of the ball facing leg. The ball should be pitched on middle and off.

Seam bowlers rely less on swing and aim to hit the pitch with the seam. The bowler would expect help from the wicket to move the ball either into or away from the batsman.

Imran Khan.

This shows the sideways movement of the ball once it has been bowled. Fast bowlers can make the ball move sideways by one side of the ball being shiny.

Outswinger aims to hit edge of bat and be caught in slips

Inswinger aims to come back in to batsman and either bowl him or get him LBW

SPIN BOWLING

**There are two basic types of spin bowling –
leg-spin and off-spin.**

LEG-SPIN BOWLING is certainly back in fashion, thanks mainly to Australia's Shane Warne, who is believed by some to be the best bowler of his type ever.

The leg-spinner usually bowls over the wicket and the ball is pitched on a good length. However, subtle variations in length and flight are vital if a leg-spinner is to succeed. The batsman should be kept guessing at all times as to what kind of delivery he is about to face.

The leg-break is a delivery that spins from leg to off after pitching. At the point of delivery the bowler uses the wrist of his bowling arm to impart the anti-clockwise spin on the ball.

The googly is a ball bowled with a leg-spinner's action but the ball spins from off to leg.

The flipper or top-spinner is a ball that goes straight on after pitching and is another weapon in the legs-pinner's armoury.

Sri Lanka's Muttiah Muralitharan and Pakistan's Saqlain Mushtaq are both world-class off-spinners and hopefully their exploits will encourage more young cricketers to take up off-spin bowling. The off-spin ball moves from off to leg and the spin is obtained by the two fingers gripping the ball twisting it clockwise at the point of delivery.

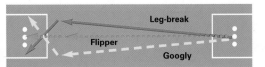

The leg-spinner has three weapons, each of which bounces approximately two feet in front of the batsman: the leg-break, the flipper and the googly.

Leg-break: bounces by the batsmen's legs and spins away

Flipper: heads straight on

Googly: bounces fast in front of the batsman and spins sharply back towards him

FINDING A TECHNIQUE

The bowler should aim to release the ball from a high position. If the pitch is not taking spin, most bowlers would bowl over the wicket. If the pitch is helpful then bowling round the wicket will create added spin and more difficulties for the batsman.

WHETHER A FAST or spin bowler, the basic ability to pitch the ball where you want it is an obvious but essential requirement; so is knowing how to deliver the type of ball that would cause most trouble to the batsman. Watch the batsman's movements when you are not bowling, assess his strengths and weaknesses, and bowl what you think are the appropriate deliveries to him.

All types of bowlers can change the type of delivery bowled by altering their grip of the ball. Keep experimenting in the nets with new grips; seek advice from coaches and experienced players.

Bowling is all about variety. A team's line-up ideally would include three pace bowlers, one leg-spinner or slow left armer (so that the stock delivery would be away from the right-handed batsman) and an off-spinner. There are many different types of bowlers and even though you may be a young fast bowler, try some leg-spinners or off-breaks in the nets. You could just be the next Shane Warne even though you had hoped to be a future Allan Donald!

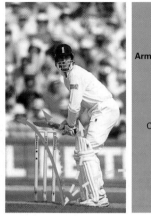

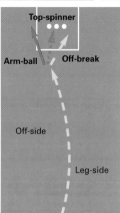

The off-spinner has three weapons also (as well as variations in flight and speed). All three deliveries start off in the same direction, making it difficult for the batsman to predict what he is facing.

Off-break, the off-spinner's usual ball, bounces on the 'off' side; spins towards the batsman's legs

Top-spinner bounces and carries straight on – bouncing a little higher than expected

Arm-ball carries on heading away from batsman: this ball doesn't spin at all; the off-spinner's version of an outswinger.

Batting

There are four basic requirements for young cricketers to master if they are to become successful batsmen. They are:

- **Grip of the bat handle**
- **Stance**
- **Backlift**
- **Footwork**

GRIP OF THE BAT HANDLE

BOTH HANDS SHOULD be close together and grip the bat tightly. Remember to use the top hand to grip the bat – many just rely on the bottom hand – a good top hand grip will give a batsman more control over his shots.

The hands should grip the bat near the top of the handle. The 'vees' between the thumbs and the first fingers should be in line and pointing somewhere between the splice and the edge of the bat. Practice your shots and change the position slightly of the 'vees' to determine which position you are happiest with.

STANCE

THE ORTHODOX STANCE is taken when a batsman takes up a sideways-on position with the left shoulder facing the

bowler and the face of the bat pointing straight back down the wicket. The feet should be either side of the popping crease and not too far apart.

Your weight should be evenly placed between the two feet. Make sure your head is held up and very still and keep your eye on the ball at all times.

There are a huge number of coaching manuals that aim to teach you how to stand at the wicket. However, many of the top players would argue the two most important features of a good stance are comfort and balance. You must feel comfortable with the way you stand and happy it is the right stance for you, personally. Perfect balance, with the ability to go forward or back with ease is also essential.

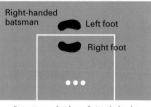

Right-handed batsman   Left foot

Right foot

Batsman stands side on, facing the bowler.

BACKLIFT

THE FIRST MOVE A batsman makes in playing any shot is the backlift. Start the backlift early so that the actual shot is not hurried at the end; let the top hand do all the work. As the bat is lifted the wrists become cocked and the bat face is opened. A good backlift should be kept as straight and fluent as possible.

There have been some extraordinary batting styles in the first-class game; some have caused controversy. Former England captain Graham Gooch adopted a very high backlift as the bowler approached but he went on to become a great Test batsman.

Carefully lift the top hand to prepare for the stroke.

FOOTWORK

GOOD FOOTWORK is vital to a batsman. He cannot execute his chosen shot without his feet being in the right position. Practice your individual shots in the nets and pay particular attention to the position of your feet. Nimble footwork will get you to the pitch of the ball if you are playing forward – either attack or defence. Good footwork when you play a shot off the back foot will give you time and room to play your blocking or forcing shot. Whether you are playing a defensive or attacking shot, you have got to be comfortable and balanced – good positioning of the feet will give you those qualities.

Play a front foot shot if the bounces near you and has not bounced up very high.

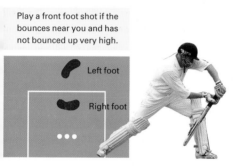

Left foot forward, right foot stays where it is.

Play this type of shot to bouncers if the ball has bounced up quite high.

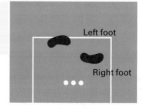

Left foot stays where it is; right comes across.

Types of Shot

DEFENSIVE SHOTS

The batsman's first priority is to defend his wicket and score runs as quickly and as regularly as he can.

IF THE BOWLER DELIVERS the perfect line and length ball, the batsman's only real option is to play a defensive shot. When a new batsman comes to the wicket it is often sensible to play defensively for an over or two in order to assess the pace of the pitch and the quality of the bowling. The state of the match and the type of innings required by you for the team should also dictate the tempo of your stay at the wicket.

Usually, a young batsman is taught how to play the forward and backward defensive shot first. The key is to keep your head still and have it directly over the ball at the moment of impact. Keep the face of the bat pointing back down the wicket.

Forward defensive shot: front foot is near where ball bounces. Ball hits bat and bounces straight down.

If the ball is on a full-length the front foot should go forward with the knee bent. The head and left shoulder should be well forward and the face of the bat kept square. The shot is controlled by the left arm, with the bat making contact with the ball level with the front foot.

Forward defensive shot: here, the ball bounces up quite high.

BACKWARD DEFENSIVE SHOT

THE BACKWARD defensive shot is played to a delivery bowled just short of a length. It is played off the back foot with the face of the bat again pointing straight back down the wicket. The ball should be watched all the way on to the bat and played down with little follow-through.

An important aspect of good defensive batting is knowing when to leave the ball alone. Many batsmen are caught behind or in the slips off the edge sparring at balls well wide of their off stump.

A defensive shot might leave you vulnerable – don't get caught behind.

ATTACKING SHOTS

THE BALL MUST be pitched up for the off-drive and its line should be on or outside the off stump. The front foot should be moved forward and be as close to the pitch of the ball as possible. The batsman's weight is then transferred to the front foot and contact made with the ball when it is level with the front foot. The face of the bat should be pointing to where you want the ball to travel. When the ball has been hit make sure you follow through.

Other attacking shots on the off side include the drive off the back foot and the cut past point or down to third man. These shots are all played to short of a length deliveries and the key is to keep the ball down. Always watch the ball onto the bat, with your head still and do not try to hit it too hard.

Attacking shot: here, the ball is heading for the camera. The direction the ball will take is indicated below right.

along the
ground

OTHER SHOTS

The on-drive is played to pitched-up balls on the leg stump and again the head should be steady and the bat facing the intended line of the shot.

THE LEG-GLANCE is another option if the bowler strays too much down the leg side. The important factor here is that the wrists turn the bat at the moment of impact in the direction of the intended shot. The leg-glance requires perfect footwork and is a good shot to practice in the nets.

The leg-glance.

Short balls on the leg-side offer the batsman the option to pull or hook. Both are risky shots and the batsman must roll his wrists as he makes contact with the ball in order to keep it down. The sweep is a dangerous shot to attempt; it is made to a slower, full-length ball outside (and sometimes on) the leg stump. The front foot comes forward to meet the ball and is then bent with the knee almost touching the ground. The ball is swept to leg with the knee almost in a horizontal position.

Runs can also be accumulated from the straight drive past mid-off or mid-on. This could be particularly useful against fast bowlers when a well-timed drive could find its way to the boundary ropes and even a gentle push back past the bowler could be worth a couple of runs.

> **Hook shot:** here, the ball bounces quite high, and is then hit at around head height
> The diagram shows direction the ball will take once batsman has hit it.

PRACTICE MAKES PERFECT

Always try to maintain your concentration. There could be interruptions to play – a drinks break, injury to a fielder or endless short breaks due to rain. Relax between deliveries and make sure you and your batting partner know and agree on the way you both should be playing for the team.

Net practice allows a player to perfect almost every part of their game.

GEOFF BOYCOTT used to practice for hours in front of a mirror so that he got his stance exactly right and gave himself the best possible chance of bringing a straight bat down on the ball.

Master batsman, Viv Richards, claims to have had little or no coaching as a youngster, and advocates strongly that budding cricketers should always be comfortable at the wicket, even if it means they go against the coach's advice. However, Richards was a one-off and we cannot all hope to bat like the former West Indies skipper.

Sir Donald Bradman became the greatest batsman of all time. When he was a schoolboy he lived in a remote farmhouse with no friends to practice his beloved cricket with. He devised his own method of practice that involved a golf ball, a single stump and a brick wall. Take a leaf out of Sir Don's book and keep practising but always remember – grip, stance, backlift and footwork.

Sir Donald Bradman.

Fielding

BACKGROUND

It is often said that bowlers win cricket matches but unless all his victims are clean-bowled or leg-before-wicket appeals are upheld, a bowler is reliant upon his fielders to be successful.

THE PRINCIPAL requirement for modern cricket is fitness, and the speed and stamina of today's fielders compares favourably with all other modern professional sports.

A clean catch.

Fielding is definitely one aspect of cricket that has improved beyond recognition in the past 30 years. Limited-overs cricket, where every run is vital, has without doubt led to

Fielders are vital to support the bowler.

the big improvement in this aspect of cricket. Before the advent of one-day cricket, specialist fielders did exist but these tended to be close-to-the-wicket fieldsmen.

Yorkshire's Phil Sharpe was rated the best First Slip in the world in the 1960s and former England star Colin Cowdrey, perhaps not the most naturally athletic of movers, excelled in the slip area. It was usually the case that fast bowlers fielded down at third man or long leg to catch their breath – rather than the ball – between overs. The more athletic players, if a side possessed them, would field in the covers and at mid-wicket.

GREAT FIELDERS

IN THE 1960s, South Africa's Colin Bland almost single-handedly raised the profile of fielding. He mesmerised crowds with his ability to swoop on the ball in the covers and take aim at a single stump and regularly break the wicket, leaving a batsman stranded. Bland was without question the most brilliant outfielder of his day and was the forerunner of a host of players who became famous as much for their fielding as their batting and bowling. Later, England's Derek Randall entertained spectators with his superb fielding and even gave demonstrations of his remarkable skills after matches had finished.

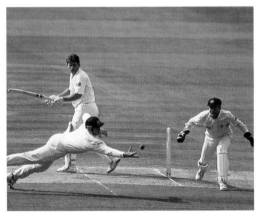

Caught out at full stretch.

CLOSE FIELDING

FIELDING CLOSE TO the wicket requires a unique approach and it is important to get your body in the right position to give yourself the best chance of catching the edged or gloved ball. Ensure you are down and well-balanced in time before the bowler lets the ball go. Most close fielders prefer to have both hands together as they crouch and wait for a catch.

Former England all-rounder, Ian Botham, was more comfortable with a hand on either knee as he crouched. But it must be pointed out that Botham was a remarkable cricketer with unusual and astonishing talents. However, most of us mortals have to be more orthodox in our approach to the game. Again, if you are in the slips it is important to watch the ball from the moment it leaves the bowler's hand.

The West Indies slips at The Oval, 1988.

FIELDING SKILLS

WHEN A YOUNG player starts to play cricket today, his fielding abilities will be scrutinised as closely by the coaches as his skills as a batsman or bowler. A cricketer will spend a long time in the field throughout his career and it is important that a young player accepts that and is prepared to work as much on improving his fielding as all other aspects of his game. A young player may find he has the reflexes to be a natural slip fieldsman, or the anticipation required to take sharp bat-pad chances at silly-point or close-in on the leg-side. Alternatively, he may be a quick runner and can cover great areas of the outfield at speed. It is important to specialise as a fielder, but it is also wise to field occasionally in other positions. This will extend a young player's range of skills and give a broader understanding of the game.

The skills required for each position are diverse but there are certain rules that relate to all fielders – close-to-the-wicket and in the outfield. One is to always keep your concentration: the ball may not come to you for long periods and it is easy to let your mind wander. Top players tend to relax between deliveries and then focus totally as the bowler begins his run-up.

Close concentration when it matters: the fielder can easily miss his moment.

A spectacular catch by Jonty Rhodes of South Africa, 1996.

FIELDERS AND THE BALL

Another common rule is always to keep your eye on the ball. This is especially important when a player is in the outfield and the ball is travelling at pace along the ground and his responsibility is to save the boundary or stop the batsmen running a second or third run. It is perhaps even more important for the outfielder to keep his eye on the ball if it has been hit in the air and he is moving, sometimes at pace, to make a catch.

A two-handed catch is safest.

IT IS EASY FOR inexperienced players to misfield a ball in their haste to get it back to the wicket-keeper. Never snatch at the ball in the field and always make sure you are in full control of it before you attempt to throw it back. In all cases it is better to gather the ball with two hands, although obviously there may be times when the ball has been hit so fast that your only hope of stopping the ball is to use one hand. When you have the ball under control, assess what you think the batsmen are about to do. If it is clear they are not going to attempt another run, make sure the ball is returned to the wicket-keeper safely and do not hurl it back for there may be a risk of giving away unnecessary overthrows.

Always reassess your tactics – unless the batsman is caught out.

FIELDERS AND THE WICKET-KEEPER

It is always best, when possible, to throw the ball to the wicket-keeper's end – he has the gloves and will be in position to gather the ball.

IF THERE IS the chance of a run-out, however, you may elect to return the ball to the bowler's end. If a side possesses a good wicket-keeper, he will inevitably shout advice to the fielder. England's Alec Stewart can often be heard during televised matches shouting 'keeper's' or 'bowler's' as a fielder gathers the ball. He also shouts 'hold it' if he thinks there is no chance of a run-out.

If you are fielding away from the wicket and the ball is driven firmly to you, go down on one knee and let your leg be a wall to stop the ball if it goes through your hands. Wherever a young player finds himself fielding, he knows he will have to perform to the best of his ability – the modern game of cricket demands it. South Africa's Jonty Rhodes is currently rated the best fielder in the world and young players should study his technique.

Fielding should no longer be seen as a chore that has to be done. Fielding can, and does, help win cricket matches.

Graeme Hick catches the ball: Worcestershire Cricket Club, 1991.

LAWS OF THE GAME
Laws and Regulations

As with most aspects of the early development of cricket, the history of the Laws is reliant on the scant documentary evidence that exists.

SOME FORM OF cricket has been played in England for centuries and the first records of matches date back to 1300. The early games were obviously played to some set of rules but the details of the playing regulations are, in most cases, sadly lost.

The earliest known regulations were issued by the London Star and Garter Club in 1755. The Marylebone Cricket Club (MCC), which was founded in 1787, soon took over responsibility for revising the Laws. Today, the MCC holds the world copyright on the Laws of Cricket.

THE 42 LAWS OF CRICKET

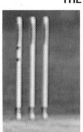

THERE ARE 42 LAWS of Cricket dealing with all aspects of play from Law One: The Players, to Law 42: Unfair Play. Cricket is a complicated game and the Rules of Cricket as published in Wisden Cricketers' Almanack take up 30 pages of the book.

The following pages attempt to explain the basic rules of the game.

Shane Warne appeals to the umpire, 1995.

Basic Rules

THE GAME

THE GAME IS played between two sides each with 11 players. Each side will have a captain, who should nominate his players before the toss. A player cannot be changed thereafter unless the opposing captain agrees. On winning the toss, a captain can elect to bat or field first.

A match can be of one or two innings according to agreement before the match.

THE EQUIPMENT

Bats

The batsman must use a bat made of wood and it shall not be more than 96.5 cm (38 in) long and 10.8 cm (4¼ in) at its widest part. Some years ago, Australian fast bowler Dennis Lillee caused a furore when he came into bat wielding a bat made of aluminium. He was told to change it and the metal bat failed to become a permanent feature of the modern game.

Stumps and bails

The wickets should be 22.9 cm (9 in) wide made up of three wooden stumps with two wooden bails on top. The stumps should be 71.1 cm

(28 in) high and sufficiently wide to prevent the ball from going between them.

The bails should be 11.1 cm (4⅜ in) in length and when on top of the stumps, should not be more than 1.3 cm (1/2 in) above them.

Balls

The ball should weigh not less than 155.9 g (5½ oz), no more than 163 g (5¾ oz). It should measure not less than 22.4 cm (8¹³/₁₆ in), nor more than 22.9 cm (9 in) in circumference.

THE MATCH

OTHER BASIC details such as the boundary edge have to be agreed before the start of play. At a county ground the boundary is clearly marked, but in village green cricket it is vital to reach agreement with the opposition on this matter.

When the match starts each bowler has six balls an over to deliver, if he is no-balled by the umpire, he has to bowl that delivery again. At the end of the over, the umpires change ends and a different bowler starts an over at the other end.

Runs

It is the job of the batsman to defend his wicket and score runs for his team. When a batsman hits the ball, he and his batting partner have to decide if they want to take a run. Normally, one, twos and threes are run. If a batsman hits the ball beyond the boundary's edge without the ball hitting the ground, he is awarded six runs. If

the ball hits the ground and then crosses the boundary, four runs are awarded.

Usually a batsman's individual total is made up of ones, twos, threes, fours and sixes. However, other figures can be shown. If he strikes the ball and it hits a fielder's helmet which has been left on the ground – usually directly behind the wicket-keeper, the umpire will signal that five runs should be awarded.

As many as seven runs could be scored if a batsman runs three and a fielder throws the ball back past his wicket-keeper to the boundary, four overthrows are added to the three run by the batsmen.

Dismissal of a Batsman

ONE OF THE most interesting sections in the Laws relates to the dismissal of a batsman. There are ten ways in which a batsman can be dismissed and asking someone to name all ten remains a popular quiz question.

1. Bowled

A batsman is out when the wicket is knocked down, even if the bat or part of his body touches the ball first. He is also out if he knocks the ball onto the wicket before completing his stroke or as a result of attempting

to defend his wicket. If the ball hits the stumps after first touching the bat it is termed 'played on', though the dismissal is still entered in the scorebook as 'bowled'.

2. Caught

If the ball touches the bat (or glove) and is caught by a fielder before hitting the ground. To be given out caught off the glove, the hand must be holding the bat at the point of impact with the ball.

3. Leg before wicket (LBW)

This is perhaps the most baffling and certainly the most contentious. The batsman is out if he fails to hit the ball and it strikes him on 'person, dress or equipment' in such a position that in the umpire's mind it would have gone on and hit the wicket. However, the ball must have pitched in a straight line between wicket and wicket or on the batsman's off-side. If the ball hits the batsman on the full and in the view of the umpire would have hit the stumps he is also out.

The most common areas liable to LBW decisions.

This is probably the hardest decision for an umpire to give. In many circumstances the batsman may feel he hit the ball before it struck his pad or that the ball would have missed the wicket anyway. Recent criticism of LBW decisions, when Test batsmen have shown open discontent and each incident shown repeatedly on televised slow motion play-backs, proves what a difficult job an umpire has.

4. Run-out

If a batsman is out of his ground when the ball is in play then he is run-out if the fielding side manage to break his wicket. He can be run-out off a no-ball if he attempts to take a run. In recent years a third umpire seated in front of a television monitor has been used at major matches. If the two umpires on the field are uncertain if a batsman was out of his ground when

the ball hit the stumps they can call for the third umpire's verdict. He will be shown slow-motion replays of the incident and give his verdict.

5. Stumped

A batsman is out if he is drawn forward, misses the delivery and the wicket-keeper collects the ball and breaks the wicket before the striker has regained his ground.

6. Hit wicket

A simple dismissal. If a batsman breaks his own wicket, either with the bat, a foot or any part of his body, in the act of playing a shot, he is out.

Clare Conner of England is stumped by Australia, 1998.

7. Handled the ball

A rare dismissal is when a batsman is given out if handles the ball when in play and does not have his hand on the bat or have the consent to do so of the opposite side. England's Graham Gooch was famously given out 'handled the ball' in the Lord's Test against Australia in 1993. He played a delivery from Merv Hughes and as the ball bounced back towards his wicket, Gooch knocked it away with his hand. The umpire, Dickie Bird, ruled that Gooch had 'wilfully' handled the ball while in play.

8. Timed out

An in-coming batsman can be given out 'timed out' on appeal by the fielding side if he 'wilfully' takes more than two minutes to arrive at the crease.

9. Hit the ball twice

Another rare type of dismissal. Law 34 states that a batsman can be dismissed 'if, after the ball has been struck or is stopped by any part of his person, he wilfully strikes it again with his bat or person except for the whole purpose of guarding his wicket'.

10. Obstructing the field

Either batsman can be given out on appeal 'if he wilfully obstructs the opposite side by word or action'. This, too, is a rare otcurrence, but there have been cases where a batsman has been given out for obstructing a ball from being caught.

Graham Gooch handles the ball and goes out, 1993.

Close of an Innings

An innings is over when ten wickets are taken by the fielding side or the last player available to bat has been dismissed. An innings can also be declared to be over by the batting captain.

AT THE END of a match, there are three possible results: a win for one of the sides (by a number of runs or wickets); a draw; or a tie.

In a match which is not restricted to a specific number of overs, a team has to capture all the opposition wickets to win, otherwise it is a draw, regardless of which side has scored the most runs.

Note: In limited-overs matches it is also possible for games to finish as a 'no result'. This happens when both sides are unable to complete a minimum number of overs necessary to achieve a result. In all other forms of cricket this result would go down in the record books as a draw.

Left: Waqar and Wasim of Pakistan after a Test win at Lord's, 1996.

Limited-overs Matches Rules

Many of the basic Laws of cricket are pertinent to the limited-overs version. There are differences, the most obvious clearly being the limitation on the number of overs allotted to either side.

WHEN THE GILLETTE CUP was launched in 1963, each side's innings lasted 60 overs. The first World Cup in 1975 allocated 55 overs per side. The normal rule nowadays in most forms of one-day knock-out cricket is for each side to bat for a maximum of 50 overs.

Restrictions on the fielding side are also unique to one-day cricket. An inner circle is drawn on a pitch and for the first 15 overs of an innings, the fielding captain must have a certain number of players within that area.

The purpose of one-day cricket is to achieve a result. There are all sorts of formulae for sides to claim a victory.

One-day cricket ensures the crowd will see a result.

If weather intervenes before a match starts, the sides can agree to play a match with a reduced number of overs. If the side batting first complete their innings but the weather prevents the side batting second from finishing all their overs, a reduced target of fewer overs can be agreed by the umpires.

Other obvious differences in the rules for one-day cricket involve equipment and kit. Players in certain major one-day matches are allowed – even encouraged by the sponsors – to wear coloured kit. A white ball is used and a black sight-screen erected to help the players see it.

Despite the transparent differences between limited-overs matches and the longer game, many of the basic Laws of Cricket apply to both version.

Coloured kit is permitted for one-day matches.

Scoring

The scorer is one of the most important people at a cricket match, be it a Test or a game on the village green. Without a true and accurate record of the match, the result – either a win, draw or tie – cannot be agreed with any real certainty.

SCORERS

NOWADAYS, THE SCORERS at first-class matches in England all carry, and operate, sophisticated laptop computers and only revert to the tried and tested book if and when the system crashes. They sit in the scorers' box and watch every delivery bowled, carefully watching for signals from the umpires. Their computers are on-line and instantaneously send data from the match to a central site for immediate dissemination to the media.

SCORING METHODS

THERE HAVE BEEN some ingenious forms of scoring over the years. In the early matches, the score was kept by cutting notches on wooden sticks. Other methods have included putting a stone in a hat or box for every run scored in an innings. When the other side went into bat, a stone was taken out for each run scored. Once the hat or box was emptied the side batting last needed one to win. If a side was all out before the hat or box was empty, the number of stones left represented the winning margin of runs.

The scoreboard operator.

DEVELOPMENT OF SCORING

The development of scoring methods in cricket is very much connected to the way the sport itself has changed over the years.

THE EARLIEST KNOWN full score from a match dates back to 1744 and records a match played between Kent and All-England at the Artillery Ground, London on 18 June of that year.

The first LBW dismissal was recorded in a match at Moulsey Hurst between Surrey and Thirteen of England in August 1795. Before that LBW dismissals were recorded as 'bowled'.

STROKE-BY-STROKE SCORING

THIS WAS INTRODUCED as early as the 1760s, although full bowling analyses were not generally recorded until the 1830s. As the rules of cricket evolved so did the scoring of matches. Wides were introduced in 1827 and no-balls, three years later. The first known scorecard for the public was printed as early as the 1776. Scorecards were printed and sold at Lord's for the first time in 1846.

SCORING TODAY

THE METHOD OF scoring cricket matches, still usually done using pen and paper, has changed little in recent years. And most scorers, from village green to senior club level would use the standard scorers' book that can be bought from high street stationers.

One of the tasks a new member of a club might be asked to undertake is that of keeping the scoreboard up to date at a match. This can involve turning over and displaying the relevant numbers on a small board showing score, wickets lost, current batsmen's scores, overs and possibly winning target.

A scoreboard shows a range of information.

SCOREBOARDS

YOU COULD find yourself inside a huge dark scorebox with just a small window to watch the play and the umpire's signals. It would be your task to keep the score up to date, and if you were a long way from the official scorers and have no telephonic link with them, the task could be onerous. It is the umpire's responsibility to ensure the official scorers have seen and acknowledged his signals, not the person pulling the levers in the scorebox.

STATISTICS

STATISTICS HAVE always played a large part in cricket. As television coverage of the game has improved so has the thirst for more facts and figures. Computer software nowadays allows the commentator to call up a host of statistics to keep the viewing public informed. It is possible to see in an instant, on-screen figures of a players' entire career that include statistics from the match you are watching. The updates are impressive and immediate. This increased access to statistics has seen newspapers and magazines look for different ways to improve their published scorecards.

Until recently scorecards printed in newspapers gave just the bare essentials: batsman's name, dismissal and runs scored (e.g. B. C. Lara c Stewart b Gough 101), number of extras, number of wickets fallen, innings total, fall of wickets and bowling figures.

The umpire's signals must be seen by official scorers.

MODERN SCORING METHODS

NOW EACH AND every detail can be enhanced. A batsman's individual innings can be broken down in terms of time at the crease; balls faced; ones, twos, three, fours, sixes scored; a description of the dismissal can be included (e.g., 'caught down leg-side trying to pull short ball to mid-wicket); extras are now also broken down to show number of no-balls, byes and leg-byes; the fall of wickets section can show the batsman dismissed (e.g. 2-198 (Lara)); bowling figures can display the different spells (e.g. Gough 12-2-24-3 (Two spells 8-2-18-3) (4-0-6-0)).

There appears an endless desire to develop different ways of displaying cricket statistics. The basic collation of the scores remains essentially the same, but methods of representing the scores will continue to evolve.

Left: Scoreboards have moved a long way from the austere lists of the 1930s, above

Positions

The field is split into two halves – an off-side
and a leg-side. The off-side is to the right of a
right-handed batsman, the leg-side to the left.
For a left-handed batsman, the off-side is to his
left and the leg-side to his right.

Wicket-keeper
Stands directly behind the
stumps. Wears pads and
gloves. Can 'stand-up' close
behind the wicket when
slower bowlers are on and
this is how he would claim
most of his stumping
dismissals. 'Stands-back',
that is, positions himself
further back from the
wickets when 'keeping to
faster bowlers.

Slips
Positioned adjacent to the wicket-keeper. The closest to the
'keeper is referred to as First Slip. The rest: Second, Third,
Fourth and Fifth Slips respectively. Their job is to catch the
edged ball.

Short or Silly mid-off/Short-extra cover
Fielders very close to the batsmen on the off. There to catch the
bat-pad chances. Close fielders are also sometimes used to
intimidate the batsman.

Point

Stands some distance from the batsman, just square of the wicket on the off. Main job is to stop quick singles being scored, and also square cuts going to the boundary. Good position for potential run-outs. Usually one of the better and more athletic fielders in the side.

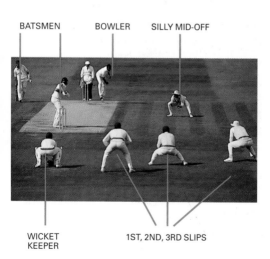

Positions around the wicket.

Gully

Stands close to the slips but wider. Also looking for the edge but can be a useful run saver if the batsman tries to hit the ball to the off and slightly behind point.

MID- ON   WICKET KEEPER   GULLY

FORWARD SHORT LEG   1ST, 2ND, 3RD SLIPS

LEG-SIDE   **OFF-SIDE**

Silly mid-on/short square-leg/short forward-leg/short backward-leg

All catching positions close in on the leg-side. There for the bat-pad chances when a ball that snicks the bat hits a pad and lobs in the air to be caught.

Cover/Extra cover

Again on the off but further round than point. Runs stoppers. There to cut-off quick singles and cover drives.

Mid-off

On the off-side but closer to the bowler. There to stop the straight drives.

Third man

Positioned on the boundary behind the wicket on the off. There to save edges or genuine late cuts from going for four. Will always concede the single but must stop twos and threes.

Long-off

A boundary fielder on the off-side positioned behind the bowler. There to stop boundaries and catch lofted drives. Will always concede the single but must stop twos and threes.

Deep point/Deep extra-cover/Deep mid-off

Point, extra-cover and mid-off pushed back to the boundary. Because they are so deep, they will always concede a single if the ball comes to them. Must stop second or third run and boundaries.

Leg-slip

Similar to First Slip but placed on the leg-side. There to catch inside edges or fine deflections off batsman's glove.

Leg-gully

Again, similar to gully but on the batsman's leg-side. Positioned for the catch off gloves and lofted leg glances.

Square-leg

A leg-side version of point. There to save the quick single and shots to the boundary. Good position for run-outs.

Mid-wicket

A leg-side version of cover. There to save the quick single and shots to the boundary. Good position for run-outs.

Mid-on

Positioned on the on-side close to the bowler. There to stop the straight drives.

Long-leg/Deep fine-leg

Positioned on the boundary behind the wicket on the on-side. There to save inside edges or genuine leg-glances from going for four. Will always concede the single but must stop twos and threes.

Long-on

A boundary fielder on the on-side positioned behind the bowler. Must stop boundaries and catch lofted drives. Will always concede the single but must stop twos and threes.

Deep square-leg/Deep mid-wicket/Deep mid-on

Point and extra-cover pushed back to the boundary. Because they are so deep they will always concede a single if the ball comes to them. Must stop second or third run and boundaries.

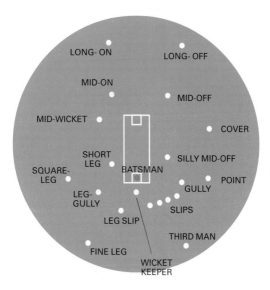

The captain has to decide on the best combination of positions for the 11-person team.

Glossary

All-rounder: A player who is worth his place in a team as a batsman or bowler. Can also describe a batsman/wicket-keeper.

Appeal: A call by a player to an umpire to decide if a batsman is out. The usual cry is: 'How's that?'.

Ashes: A trophy played for by England and Australia. At the end of each Test series, the winning side 'holds the Ashes'. The actual trophy is a small, wooden urn and is said to contain the ashes of a bail.

Averages: Statistics relating to a team's, or individual player's, performance.

Back up, to: When a fielder stands behind a wicket-keeper or other player to prevent overthrows if the ball is not gathered safely when it is returned from the outfield.

Ball: The object for the batsman to hit. Usually made with an outer layer of stitched leather dyed red

(white balls are now used in day/night one-day matches).

Bat: The instrument used by the batsman to hit the ball. The blade must be made of wood and not be more than 4 ¼ inches in width.

Beamer: A fast, head-high delivery which is now forbidden under Law 42.

Blue: A 'Blue' is awarded to a player when he plays for either Cambridge or Oxford University.

Bosie: Australian term for a leg-spinner's googly – derives from inventor of googly, B. J. T. Bosenquet.

Bouncer: A fast short-pitched delivery that is aimed to reach a batsman at shoulder height or higher.

Box: A shield for protecting the private parts of a batsman, wicket-keeper or close-in fielder.

Bump ball: When a ball is hit straight into the ground by a batsman and the ball bounces up for a fielder to take a 'catch'.

Bumper: A fast-short ball (same as Bouncer).

Bye: A run scored when the ball has missed the batsman without touching his bat or any part of his body.

Call: A call by a batsman to his partner to run (or not to run).

Cap: A cricketer's headgear. At county cricket level, a 'capped' player is one who has been awarded his county First XI cap. At Test level a player is awarded a 'cap' for every match played.

Carry one's bat: When an opening batsman remains unbeaten when the 10th wicket of an innings is taken.

Castle: Colloquial term for wicket. 'Castled' refers to a batsman being bowled.

Chinaman: A left-arm spinner's off-break to a right-hand batsman.

Chucker: Bowler who delivers the ball illegally by throwing it instead of bowling it, as laid down in Law 24.

Close field: Fielding positions close to the wicket.

Closure: Declaration of an innings

Cut: A stroke with a horizontal bat to a short-pitched delivery on the off-side.

Declaration: The closing of an innings by a team's captain when there are still wickets to fall.

Deep: The area of the field near to the boundary

Donkey drop: A ball bowled high in the air and slowly to a batsman.

Duck: A score of nought.

Extras: Runs added to a total not made by a batsman (These can be byes, leg-byes, wides, no-balls).

First-class cricket: The highest standard of matches outside Test cricket.

Flipper: A type of ball bowled by a leg-spinner. The ball hurries on to a batsman after pitching.

Follow-on: When a side finishes more than 150 runs behind the opposition's first innings (200 runs in Test matches), it can be asked by the opposing to bat again out of order.

Follow-through: The path a bowler takes after he has let go of the ball.

Full toss: A delivery that reaches a batsman on the full.

Gardening: When a batsman repairs a part of the pitch that has been damaged by impact with the ball.

Glance: A deflection of the ball off the face of the bat, usually down the leg-side.

Googly: An off-break delivery bowled with a leg-spinner's action.

Gully: A close fielder on the off-side between slips and point.

Half-volley: An over-pitched delivery that allows the batsman to hit it on the front foot just after it has bounced.

Hat-trick: Feat of taking three wickets in three balls.

How's that?: Standard form of appeal from fielder to umpire to claim a batsman's dismissal.

King pair: Refers to a batsman who has been dismissed first ball in both innings of a match.

Leg break: A delivery that turns from leg to off after pitching.

Leg-bye: A run obtained when a batsman unintentionally misses a ball with his bat and it is deflected off his body.

Long hop: A short-pitched delivery easily played by the batsman – usually by cutting or pulling for runs.

Maiden over: An over from which no runs are scored by the batsman. Byes and leg-byes can be scored and the bowler is still credited with having bowled a 'maiden'.

Night-watchman: A lower-order batsman sent in towards the end of a day's play on the fall of a wicket rather than risk a more talented player at that stage of the proceedings. His job is to bat out time and let the more gifted batsmen come in the following day.

No-ball: An illegal delivery. If a no-ball is called by the umpire, the bowler has to bowl another delivery even if runs have been scored of the illegal ball.

Off-break: A ball that turns from off to leg when it has pitched.

Off-drive: Offensive shot by batsman between cover and mid-off.

On-drive: Offensive drive by batsman between mid-wicket and mid-on.

Overthrows: When a ball is returned from the outfield and is not gathered cleanly and allows the batsman to take additional runs.

Pair: When a batsman scores nought in both innings of a match.

Pinch hitter: Term borrowed from baseball. A hard-hitting batsman who is sent in early in an innings to score quick runs.

Played on: When a batsman deflects the ball off his bat and onto his wicket.

Return: A throw to the stumps at either end after the ball has been fielded.

Rubber: A number of Tests played by two countries in the same season. Also known as a 'series'.

Runner: A member of the batting side who is allowed to run for a batsman who has been injured during the match.

Score book: The book of printed forms on which match details are recorded.

Seam: The stitching around the circumference of the ball that keeps the leather sections fastened. This is very important to the various techniques employed by bowlers.

Session: One of the three sections of a day's play. Morning session (before lunch); afternoon session (after lunch and before tea) and evening session (after tea to close of play).

Short-leg: Fielder close in on the leg-side.

Short run: Called by an umpire when a batsman does not make his ground at one end in attempting two or more runs. The run is not added to the total.

Slip: Close fielding position on the off adjacent to the wicket-keeper.

Swerve: Old term for swing and describes the lateral movement of a delivery.

Tail: Lower order batsman not selected for their batting skills.

Test match: Match played over five days by countries who are full members of the International Cricket Conference.

Toss: When the two captains get together before a match starts to decide who is going to bat first. A coin is tossed in the air by the home captain and the away skipper shouts 'heads' or 'tails'. Whoever wins the toss has the choice of batting or fielding first.

Twelfth man: Substitute fieldsman.

Wicket maiden: An over in which no runs are scored, but a wicket has fallen that has been credited to the bowler.

Yorker: A full-pitched ball that beats a batsman stroke and goes underneath the bat.

Useful Addresses

England and Wales Cricket Board, Lord's Cricket Ground, London NW8 8QZ. Tel. 0171 4320 1200. Fax. 0171 289 5619.

International Cricket Council, The Clock Tower Lord's Cricket Ground, London NW8 8QZ.

Minor Counties Cricket Association, Thorpe Cottage, Mill Common, Ridlington, North Walsham NR28 9TY. Tel. 01692 650563.

Association of Cricket Umpires and Scorers, PO Box 399, Camberley, Surrey GU16 5ZJ. Tel. 01276 27962.

English Schools' Cricket Association, 38 Mill House, Woods Lane, Cottingham, Hull, HU16 4HQ.

Women's Cricket Association, Warwickshire County Cricket Ground, Edgbaston Road, Birmingham B5 7QX. Tel. 0121 440 0567. Fax/Answerphone: 0121 440 0520.

Bibliography

Sir Donald Bradman: The Art of Cricket by Sir Donald Bradman, (Robson Books. 1958, revised 1998) *The Skills of Cricket* by Keith Andrew, (The Crowood Press. 1984, revised 1989) *Playfair Cricket Annual,* Editor: Bill Frindall, (Headline Book Publishing. Various years) *The Cricketers' Who's Who* 1998, Editor: Chris Hawkins, (Queen Anne Press. 1998) *Benson & Hedges Cricket Year,* Editor: David Lemmon, (Bloomsbury Publishing. Various years) *W. G. Grace: A Life* by Simon Rae, (Faber & Faber. 1998) *Cricket Rules: A Player's Guide* by Tom Shepherd, (Blandford. 1995. Revised 1997) *The Rise of West Indian Cricket: From Colony to Nation* by Frank Birbalsingh, (Hansib Publishing. 1996) *The Spirit of Cricket: A Personal Anthology,* Christopher Martin-Jenkins, (Faber & Faber. 1994) *Wisden Cricketer's Almanack,* Editor: Matthew Engel, (John Wisden. Various years).

Index